CHRISTIAN WORLDVIEW FOR STUDENTS VOL. II

YOUR WORLDVIEW NOTES FOR
GOING TO COLLEGE WITHOUT GOING ASTRAY

BRANNON HOWSE
President and Founder of Worldview Weekend

CHRISTIAN WORLDVIEW FOR STUDENTS
VOL II
YOUR WORLDVIEW NOTES FOR
GOING TO COLLEGE WITHOUT GOING ASTRAY
Published by Worldview Weekend Publishing
a division of Worldview Weekend

© 2008 by Brannon Howse
International Standard Book Number:
0-9785014-6-2

Cover Design by
Joe Potter

For Information:
www.worldviewweekend.com

Printed in the United States of America

CONTENTS

INTRODUCTION

On Being Sorry, Not Saved

In several books, from the Worldview Weekend platform, and in various articles, I've sounded the alarm about the sorry state of the worldviews of many evangelical Christians. Numerous studies—perhaps the most stunning of which was done by the Southern Baptist Church of its own youth—reveal that the lifestyles, the values, and the resulting worldviews of most of those who attend "evangelical churches" are no different from those of the world. What's more, a large majority of students leave the church after graduating from high school, never to return.

While the studies reveal the problem, they don't explain what has caused it, but I believe I know. The root is that our churches are filled with false converts. And it's a problem I identify with all too readily because—despite being raised in a Christian home, attending a Christian school, and becoming a member of a Bible-believing church—I was a false convert myself until I was an adult. And the scary part is that it's not all that hard to do!

I played the "game" (even though I didn't know I was playing a game). I thought I was saved because I believed in Jesus Christ, had prayed the "sinner's prayer," walked the aisle, and been baptized. I was "sorry" for my sins, but it was not the kind of sorrow that produces repentance unto salvation. After searching the Scriptures further, I discovered the source of my dysfunctional attempt at Christianity in 2 Corinthians 7: 9-10:

5

Now I rejoice, not that you were made sorry, but that your sorrow led to repentance. For you were made sorry in a godly manner, that you might suffer loss from us in nothing. For godly sorrow produces repentance leading to salvation, not to be regretted; but the sorrow of the world produces death.

True repentance was missing from my heart and, hence, from my life! "Godly sorrow" causes someone to turn and go in the opposite direction of a willfully sinful life. True repentance leads to a change in a person's life, priorities, and desires, and it produces God-honoring fruit.

You see, many people say they believe in Jesus, but this does not make them saved. Recall that the Bible says demons believe in Jesus (James 2:19), but so what? It's not a saving belief.

Too often people say they're saved because they're sorry for the bad things they do, but they continue to willfully live a life marked more by disobedience (sin), than a life of obedience (righteousness). The 2 Corinthians passage makes clear that there is a worldly sorrow that leads to death and a godly sorrow that produces repentance leading to salvation.

What really caught my attention and caused me to realize I was not a good person, that I was totally depraved and deserved hell, was when I encountered the Biblical teaching and doctrine of the moral law or the Ten Commandments. *That* made me realize only a godly sorrow leading to repentance and salvation would do. The moral law revealed my true condition—my extreme sinfulness and depravity.

Sadly, repentance is *not* a Christian doctrine we hear taught often enough (many churches never teach it), and as a result, the church is filled with false converts. This dire reality should concern all of us. Scripture is forthright about how important this is:

- The word "repent" and its various forms are used over 100 times in the Bible.
- John the Baptist preached in the wilderness, "Repent, for the kingdom of heaven is at hand!" (Matthew 3:2).
- Jesus preached this same message of repentance. Mark 1: 14, 15 says, "Now after John was put in prison, Jesus came to Galilee, preaching the gospel of the kingdom of God, and saying, 'The time is fulfilled, and the kingdom of God is at hand. Repent, and believe the gospel.'"
- In Mark 6, Jesus sends out the 12 disciples, two by two. Verse 12 states, "So they went out and preached that people should *repent*" (italics mine).

Every day 150,000 people step off into eternity, and a frightening percentage of them fall into eternal judgment. Many who wind up under judgment are likely shocked when they realize their situation. They will have thought they lived a good life as defined by today's standards. They went to church, perhaps even walked the aisle and got baptized. Some even taught Sunday school. But Jesus warned this would happen:

Not everyone who says to me, "Lord, Lord," will enter the kingdom of heaven, but the one who does the will of my Father who is in heaven. On that day many will say to me, "Lord, Lord, did we not prophesy in your name, and cast out demons in your name, and do many mighty works in your name?" And then will I declare to them, "I never knew you; depart from me, you workers of lawlessness." (Matthew 7:21-23)

I thank God someone once spoke doctrine into my life, revealed the true condition of my heart and mind, and declared "code blue" for my soul. It's time for the American church to declare "code blue" and return to teaching sound Biblical doctrine—to our children, teens *and* adults—because hearts and minds are at eternal risk.

In case, you're wondering what some of the key issues are about which to understand the Biblical worldview, that's the purpose of this book. This second *Christian Worldview for Students* will get you a good deal further down the road of understanding and prepare you in even deeper ways to stand up for the only thoroughly rational worldview—and the only one that can assure you of an eternal life to ponder it all.

THE BELIEF SYSTEM YOU CAN BELIEVE IN

1

The Most Important True/False Test You'll Ever Take

The late Dr. Francis Schaeffer was one of the greatest defenders of the Christian faith in the 20th Century. He predicted the American church would become inconsequential because of a false concept of spirituality. Self-professing Christians would talk about God and proclaim a belief in God while rejecting the God of the Bible—instead following a man-made New Age god.

I believe one of the main reasons we have a crisis in the American church, that Christians poll no differently from the world, and that students are leaving the church in large numbers is that we have an epidemic of false converts within the American church. Many people today call themselves Christians but do not believe in many, if any, of the essential Christian doctrines.

My own study of the Old Testament moral law revealed to me that I was not a good person, but it was when I opened the book of 1 John, took a pen, and underlined every sign of a true convert that I realized I did not meet even half of them. To my dismay, I recognized myself as a false convert.

First John 5:13 tells why the book of 1 John was written: "These things I have written to you who believe in the name of the Son of God, that you may *know* that you have eternal life" (emphasis mine).

Here are 1 John's ten signs of a true convert (you might want to compare yourself to make sure you're where you think you are):

1. A true convert admits he or she is a sinner. He does not believe he can go to heaven by being a "good" person. She understands her own totally depravity. (1 John 1:8)

2. A true convert lives a life of obedience by keeping God's commandments more often than breaking them. A true convert is not a habitual sinner. There's a difference between stumbling into sin and jumping in with both feet. While true converts may continue to sin as part of the struggle with our sin nature, the life of a true convert is marked by a desire to pursue holiness and walk in obedience to God's Word. (1 John 2:3-6, 3:6, 5:2)

3. A true convert does not harbor hate for his brother but displays forgiveness, love, and compassion. (1 John 2:9, 2:11, 3:15, 4:16, 4:20)

4. A true convert does not love the world or the things of the world, nor the world's system of evil, ruled by Satan. (1 John 2:15)

5. A true convert proclaims Jesus Christ as the Son of God and defends the exclusivity of Christ in a world of multiple religious systems. (1 John 4:15)

6. A true convert hopes and longs for the return of the Lord. (1 John 3:2-3)

7. A true convert desires to serve and help other Christians. (1 John 3:17, 3:14)

8. A true convert loves being with other believers and hearing the Word taught. (1 John 5:1)

9. A true convert rejects false teaching. (1 John 2:22-23)

10. A true convert remains in the truth and perseveres in the faith. (1 John 2:24)

The following e-mail reveals that when we are faithful to proclaim truth and what it really means to be a Christian, people like Nick (and me!) will listen, open God's Word, be convicted, and come to a place of godly sorrow that produces repentance unto salvation.

Dear Mr. Howse,

I took your worldview test a few years ago and ranked as a secular humanist worldview thinker. At the time, I got mad at it and mad at your organization. I took the test again just a few weeks ago and ranked as a strong Biblical worldview thinker. I knew I'd changed vastly in recent times, but never how much. I've become a new man since those few years back, and I'm happy for it.

I was raised by a Lutheran father and non-denominational Christian mother. I'd always been a strong believer in God's existence and the salvation found in Christ. However, I realize now that I never really understood it during all of those years. Even though I accepted the Bible as truth, looking back I realize how much I twisted meaning to find what I wanted to see instead of what was there. This "liberal theology" is due a lot, I believe, to the media and societal structure in which we live. I have seen many, many others fall victim to it, as well as false doctrines such as theistic evolutionism. Thankfully, those misinterpretations are in my past, and I now stand with the real truth in hand.

I attend one of the largest evangelical churches in the Las Vegas area. As I silently observe my college contemporaries, I see that they are like I once was—having a terribly skewed interpretation of God's Word or in many cases, even worse, they deny the Lord outright. Watching this, along with an even greater passion for the lost, inspired me to begin studying for the ministry. I'd spent about 12 years of my life preparing for and gearing towards becoming an attorney. Now, all I want to do is spread the message of our Lord.

In any case, I just wanted to let you know how much I've changed and how much more Biblical I've become. Praise the Lord for that.

Sincerely,
Nick

Remember, your faithfulness to proclaim truth may very well assist someone in passing the true/false converts test once and for all.

2

DOCTRINE'S NOT BORING
BUT A STRONG MOORING

I spoke to the teens in our church youth group for a series of four Sunday nights, and the youth pastor expected only about 15 students to show up for this Biblical worldview training. Happily, though, 43 showed up the first night and stayed with us all four weeks. In fact, at the end of the series, many of the students asked if I would conduct another similar series in the future.

My experience suggests that young people are hungry for sound, Biblical doctrine, but why else is it so important that we teach teens (and adults) Biblical doctrine?

1. Biblical doctrine builds discernment and reveals the will of God for our lives.

- Discernment. "But test everything, hold fast what is good" (1 Thessalonians 5:21). "Do not be conformed to this world, but be transformed by the renewal of your mind, that by testing you may discern what is the will of God, what is good and acceptable and perfect" (Romans 12:2).

- The will of God. "If anyone wills to do His will, he shall know concerning doctrine, whether it is from God or whether I speak on My own authority" (John 7:17).

2. Biblical doctrine prepares us for good works.

"All Scripture is given by the inspiration of God, and is profitable for doctrine, for reproof, for correction, for instruction in righteousness, that the man of God may be complete, thoroughly equipped for every good work" (2 Timothy 3:16-17).

3. There has been a vast falling away from Biblical truth.

"For the time will come when they will not endure sound doctrine, but according to their own desires, because they have itching ears, they will heap up for themselves teachers; and they will turn their ear away from truth and be turned aside to fables" (2 Timothy 4:3-4).

4. False teaching is destroying lives.

"Beware lest anyone cheat you through philosophy and empty deceit, according to the tradition of men, according to the basic principles of the world, and not according to Christ" (Colossians 2:8).

5. Biblical doctrine taught early and consistently builds a faith that lasts.

Paul, speaking about Timothy, says, "And that from childhood you have known the Holy Scriptures, which are able to make you wise for salvation through faith which is in Christ Jesus" (2 Timothy 3:15).

"You shall teach them diligently to your children, and shall talk of them when you sit in your house, when you walk by the way, when you lie down, and when you rise up" (Deuteronomy 6:7).

6. Biblical doctrine stirs the heart and mind.

Proverbs 4:23 explains that out of the heart "spring the issues of life."

"For with the heart one believes unto righteousness, and

with the mouth confession is made unto salvation" (Romans 10:10).

7. There is no application without acquisition—knowledge means the acquisition of truth; wisdom means the application of truth.

"For the Lord gives wisdom; from his mouth come knowledge and understanding" (Proverbs 2: 6). "The fear of the Lord is the beginning of wisdom" (Proverbs 9:10).

8. Biblical doctrine convicts those who contradict.

"Holding fast the faithful word as he has been taught that he may be able, by sound doctrine, both to exhort and convict those who contradict" (Titus 1:9).

10. Biblical doctrine will last forever.

The Bible says that "the grass withers and the flower fades," but the Word of God stands forever (Isaiah 40:7). When we commit ourselves to teaching and training hearts and minds with the Word of God, we are planting in the lives of others something that will last through all eternity.

11. Lives are at stake, and it is appointed unto every man to die once and then face judgment.

"Brethren, if any among you wanders from the truth, and someone turns him back, let him know that he who turns a sinner from the error of his way will save a soul from death and cover a multitude of sins" (James 5:19-20).

Adults as well as teens can tell you all about pop culture, about sports teams and superstars, but can they tell you how we know Jesus is God, how we know the Bible is true, or how we know Jesus rose from the dead? Biblical doctrine is the Gospel, the will of God for our lives, and it is what Jesus talked most about during His earthly ministry. Should we do any less?

3

What Sets the Bible Apart?

The Bible has an amazing pedigree. Despite being penned by more than 40 authors from some 20 different walks of life during a time span of centuries, it presents a consistent message from beginning to end.1 Why? Because the writers penned the Bible as they were led by God..

The Christian belief in the supernatural quality of the Bible is a reasonable conclusion, given the book's background. Theologian and Biblical scholar F. F. Bruce explains:

> The Bible, at first sight, appears to be a collection of literature—mainly Jewish. If we inquire into the circumstances under which the various biblical documents were written, we find that they were written at intervals over a space of nearly 1400 years.
>
> The writers wrote in various lands, from Italy in the west to Mesopotamia and possibly Persia in the east. The writers themselves were a heterogeneous number of people, not only separated from each other by hundreds of years and hundreds of miles, but belonging to the most diverse walks of life.
>
> In their ranks we have kings, herdsmen, soldiers, legislators, fishermen, statesmen, courtiers, priests and prophets, a tent-making rabbi, and a Gentile physician....not to speak of others of whom we know nothing apart from the writings they have left us.
>
> The writings themselves belong to a great variety of

literary types. They include history, law (civil, criminal, ethical, ritual, sanitary), religious poetry, didactic treatise, lyric poetry, parable and allegory, biography, personal correspondence, personal memoirs and diaries, in addition to the distinctively biblical types of prophecy and apocalyptic.

For all that, the Bible is not simply an anthology; there is a unity that binds the whole together. An anthology is compiled by an anthologist, but no anthologist compiled the Bible.[2]

The fulfillment of prophecy is also evidence of the supernatural character of God's Word. You may be fascinated to know that the Bible predicted a number of modern issues thousands of years ago:

• Evolution accepted instead of Creationism—2 Peter 3:5-6;

• Technological explosion that includes a huge growth in knowledge, speed of transportation, and worldwide communications—Daniel 12:4, Matthew 24:30, Nahum 2:3-4, Amos 8:11-13 and Revelation 11:7.

Consider a few facts about technological development that could not possibly—from a simply human standpoint—have been anticipated by Biblical writers:

• In the last 50 years there has been more scientific progress than in the previous 5,000 years.

• Ninety percent of all scientists who ever lived are alive today.

- Before 1830 people traveled on foot, by horse, or in sailing ships. From 1830 to 1890, the steam engines gave us trains and ships. From 1890 to today, we have seen the creation of automobiles, planes, jets, and spacecraft that have taken us to the moon. We have even landed unmanned spacecrafts on Mars.

- Thanks to satellites, telephones, and the Internet we have real-time worldwide communications.

As a special case, the nation of Israel clearly points to the uniqueness of Scripture. The Bible foretold Israel would again become a nation, and in 1948 that came to pass just as predicted more than 2,000 years ago (Ezekiel 36 and 37). Scripture even goes into great detail about what modern Israel would be like:

- Its form of money—the shekel (Ezekiel 45:12).

- Jewish people would come to Israel from the four corners of the earth (Ezekiel 37:16-17).

- The official language—Hebrew (Zephaniah 3:9). Today, daily newspapers in Israel are printed in Hebrew.

- The desert of Israel will become like a garden (Ezekiel 36:26-35 and Isaiah 27:6). Israeli farmers now produce four to six times what an average farmer in America produces. In particular, Israel exports tons of fruit and flowers to other countries, hardly typical desert fare.

- Israel will have a great army (Ezekiel 37:10), and

as the world has seen many times since 1948, Israel's military and intelligence agency is an extraordinary force to be reckoned with.

Far from not being special in any way, the Bible is actually special in so many ways there are whole libraries of books to back up that claim. But perhaps this overview will get your truth muscles toned a bit.

4

WHY NOT EVERYONE GOES TO HEAVEN

Most followers of the New Age Movement, also known as Cosmic Humanism, don't believe in heaven or hell, but in reincarnation—the belief that a person's soul repeatedly passes from one body to another at death. The process continues until the soul reaches a state of perfection when the soul's good karma (good deeds) outweighs its bad karma (bad deeds). The pay-off for good karma is a soul reincarnated into a desirable state. The alternative is, not surprisingly, a less desirable state.

An inconsistency arises, though, when you discuss "good" and "bad" karma. According to New Agers, there is no right or wrong, only interaction of forces. Dostoevsky points out, "Anything is permissible if there is no God, but anything is also permissible if everything is God."[3] The very process the belief system supports requires that some things are better than others—otherwise, who's to know whether someone's karma is good or not. In order to have good and bad karma, there must be a standard by which to determine what is good and what is bad. This is just one of many contradictions within New Age philosophy.

New Age leader J.Z. Knight claims to have a 35,000-year-old spirit that speaks or channels through her. On the ABC News program 20/20, Knight claimed, "If you believe in reincarnation, how could murder be wrong? If someone is murdered, it happened because they wanted it to happen, or their bad karma caught up with them." (Just for the record: I submit that J.Z. Knight is not channeling a 35,000-year-old spirit but a demon from the dark side of the spiritual world.)

Similarly, New Ager Kevin Ryerson says killers can actually turn out to be great people, thanks to reincarnation:

> Criminals and murderers sometimes come back around to be murdered themselves, or perhaps to become a saint. For instance, Moses was a murderer.... He beat the fellow to death out of rage, which was not exactly the most ethical decision. But he went on to become a great intellect, a great law-giver, and is considered a saint by many people. So basically, you get many chances. Your karma is your system of judgment. There is justice.[4]

A look at the inconsistencies in this one paragraph points out again why "earning points" to get to heaven—or to achieve a better reincarnation or whatever afterlife reward you choose—just doesn't wash. Ryerson claims Moses did not act ethically when killed the Egyptian for beating an Israelite slave. But how could a New Ager judge the actions of Moses as unethical if there is no personal judging and no absolute standard? Ryerson also says karma is "your system of judgment," and "there is justice." If there are no absolutes—if evil and good are all part of each other because all is part of God and God is part of everything—then an idea such as "justice" has no meaning.

The more you read and listen to New Agers, the more you realize they talk in circles and contradict themselves every time they go around. They're really getting nowhere—let alone to heaven.

EDUCATION
IN NAME ONLY

5

Education as Humanist Worldview Training
Lesson 1

The great American "hero" of public education, John Dewey—along with other "heroes" like Karl Marx, Aldous Huxley, B. F. Skinner, and Benjamin Bloom—promoted the idea that a student's academic achievement matters only if it in some way benefits the state. Of course, before a student's learning can be put to use for the good of all, his or her attitudes, values, feelings, and beliefs must be conformed to what the state wants. In his book, *My Pedagogic Creed*, Dewey proclaimed:

> I believe that the school is primarily a social institution….The teacher's business is simply to determine, on the basis of the larger experience and riper wisdom, how the discipline of life shall come to the child…. All these questions of the grading of the child and his promotion should be determined by reference to the same standard. Examinations are of use only so far as they test the child's fitness for social life.[5]

In other words, the goal of school is to determine where students fit in the social and economic hierarchy—the modernist version of a caste system. Sound crazy? Well, it is, but that hasn't stopped our left-leaning officials from putting as much of the concept to work as possible.

Today's Outcome-Based Education test is used to determine how a child's attitudes, values, and feelings line up with the state's preferences. In 1997, Governor Roy Romer of Colorado, while serving as a board member of the Goals 2000 panel, was asked how to enforce national standards. Romer replied:

> I believe if you were to get all employers of this country saying that we would not hire anybody unless we see a high school graduate certificate that has on it the results of this potential employee's record....Then I think this nation will come to the realization that there is no job for them, there is no life for them....There is the motivation.[6]

The governor believes in coercing Americans to line up for state inspection!

Chester Finn, former assistant secretary of education and one of the authors of Goals 2000, has recommended a system of rewards and punishments based on federal government standards:

> Perhaps the best way to enforce this standard is to confer valuable benefits and privileges on people who meet it, and to withhold them from those who do not. Work permits, good jobs and college admission are the most obvious, but there is ample scope here for imagination in devising carrots and sticks. Drivers licenses could be deferred, so could eligibility for professional athletic teams. The minimum wage paid to those who earn their certificates [of mastery] might be a dollar higher.[7]

In a truly scary adaptation of the plan on May 23, 1996, *The Cincinnati Post* reported:

Adults have credit cards and money cards. But soon, students in Cincinnati public schools will have a special card of their own and what it could buy them is their future in the world of work. The "smart card," proposed by Procter & Gamble Chairman John Pepper, is expected to be in the hands of ninth-graders, and possibly seventh-graders, by the start of the next school year. Equipped with a computer chip, the card will contain a cumulative record of the student's grades, attendance, proficiency, test scores, extra-curricular activities, athletics and other accomplishments. By the time the student graduates, the card should contain all the pertinent information a prospective employer needs about the applicant. All employers would ask to see the Smart Card and preference would be given to those with good performance.[8]

If the "Big Brother" implications of that idea don't alarm you, then let me spell it out. Consider what might be considered "good performance" in the eyes of the state: The standards could be tied to how politically correct your thinking is.

If the idea of a scholastic smart card sounds familiar, you may have seen a report in the March 16, 1992, *New York Times International* which explained a sinister-sounding plan in China, the world's role-model for denial of personal liberties:

a file is opened on each urban citizen when he or she enters elementary school and it shadows the person throughout life, moving on to high school, college, employer.... The dangan contains political evaluations that affect career prospects.... The file is kept by one's employer. The dangan affects promotions and job opportunities.... Any prospective employer is supposed to examine an applicant's dangan before making hiring decisions.[9]

China confers a noble-sounding name on their education process: life-long learning. What it means, though, is life-long monitoring and oppression by the state. Unfortunately, people don't recognize the same menacing potential in our governmental education plans here in the United States.

In 1977, U.S. Assistant Secretary of Education Mary Francis Barry said America is embarking on an education reform movement based on the four pillars of the Chinese model:

(1) Eliminate tests and grades;

(2) Make truth a relative concept;

(3) Educate to serve the masses;

(4) Merge education with labor.

We're basing our education on the Chinese model? When did following the lead of Communist China become a good idea? The last time I checked, it was our Constitution that included a Bill of Rights—not theirs.

6

EDUCATION AS HUMANIST WORLDVIEW TRAINING

LESSON 2

I n Las Vegas Darcy Tucker was pulled out of a geography class—without parental consent—to be given a computerized assessment of career possibilities. Although she aspires to become a veterinarian, the computer said Darcy ought to be a bartender or waitress, and it spat out a list of courses she should take to that end. Darcy's mother said, "The school stepped on my toes as a parent. It is my job to direct my child's career path, and it would not be in her best interest to be a bartender."[10] It might be in Nevada's best interest—given the insatiable hospitality needs of the gambling and entertainment industry—but not Darcy's.

In his classic story of government oppression, *Brave New World*, Aldous Huxley explained this motivation for government control:

> ...we require....enabling government managers to assign any given individual to his or her proper place in the social and economic hierarchy. Round pegs in square holes tend to have dangerous thoughts about the social system and to infect others with their discontents.[11]

In other words, those who do not agree with the state's worldview ("standards") will not be allowed to pursue positions of power or influence either socially or economically. And this standards testing is now in progress. Among 100 true/false questions included in a career exploration test used in six states are these:

- I have taught a Sunday school class or otherwise take an active part in my church;

- I believe in a God who answers prayers;

- I pray to God about my problems;

- I read the Bible or other religious writings regularly;

- I believe in life after death;

- I believe that God created man in His own image;

- If I ask God for forgiveness, my sins are forgiven.

While it could be argued that such questions help determine a student's fitness for a career in Christian ministry, it does not take much imagination to see how they could be equally well used to screen someone out of certain occupations in the name of finding the "proper place" to assign each student.

Mark Tucker is president of the National Center on Education and the Economy, an organization that has led the charge in passing school-to-work legislation at the state and federal levels. In the February 4, 1998, issue of *Education Week*, Millicent Lawton quoted Tucker as encouraging government control of individual destinies:

> State higher education systems would deny admission to those who didn't have the certificate [of mastery], and state leaders would prod employers to express a preference for hiring job applicants who had the certificate. Both conditions would serve as powerful incentives for students.[12]

This sort of thinking has troubling roots. Whether socialist, communist or Marxist, the foundation of all these philosophies is the humanist worldview. In his book, *Character and Destiny*, Dr. D. James Kennedy explains:

> Humanists are socialists by nature. Like Karl Marx, they see private property as primitive and selfish, nationalism and pride of country as dangerous, and allegiance to any power other than the socialist state should be illegal. Ideas, ethics, and the means of production belong to the state. For supporters such as Paul Kurtz, B.F. Skinner, John Dewey, Francis Crick, Isaac Asimov, and the other signers of the [humanist] manifesto, communism and state socialism were the only logical solutions to mankind's problems. In the first edition of that thin volume, they wrote, "A socialized and cooperative economic order must be established to the end that the equitable distribution of the means of life be possible…"

Whether Outcome-Based Education, certificates of mastery, the strengthening of federally controlled schools, or attacking the traditional family and its associated private property rights, private schools, and home schools, humanists have one ultimate goal: the creation of a humanistic, socialistic nation where everything is shared, everyone is the same, and the ruling class controls life in whatever ways it chooses. And it all seems to start in the classroom.

7

WHY SCHOOL-TO-WORK DOESN'T WORK
LESSON 1

My friend Michael Reagan once pointed out to me that former Florida governor Jeb Bush was the first governor in America to sign into law a state-wide requirement that ninth-grade high school students pick a career major and focus on that major from ninth through twelfth grade. I had predicted this on his radio show numerous times over the course of about a dozen years and also in a book for which he wrote the foreword.

As the education reporter and frequent guest host of the "Michael Reagan Program," I had spent countless hours discussing Goals 2000, School-to-Work, Outcome-Based Education, HR6, No Child Left Behind, and numerous other pieces of federal legislation that were attempting to merge education with industrial production and turn our schools in vocational centers where students are "trained" instead of educated. Republicans and Democrats are both to blame for nailing down this concept from the tenth plank of the Communist Manifesto—which includes "combination of education with industrial production"—right here in the good old U.S. of A.

Starting in 1992, America's schools have been gradually transformed into vocational centers instead of halls of learning. T.G. Stict, who served under Secretary of Labor Robert Reich, has said, "Many companies have moved operations to places with cheap, relatively poorly educated labor. What may be crucial, they say, is the dependability of a labor force and how well it can be managed and trained, not its general education level."

Through school-to-work the "State" decides which children go on to college and which go on to work following "training certification." After reviewing a student's educational history or portfolio, Big Brother State determines the career track or job the individual is to pursue. The State's desires take precedence over the wishes of the individual and his or her parents. Those who have conformed to the federal and state "standards" will be rewarded with further education and a good job. Those who do not meet the liberal and Secular Humanist worldview will likely be pushed to vocational jobs where they can have little impact on the culture with their Christian worldview.

President George H. W. Bush gave us America 2000, and then President Bill Clinton changed the name to Goals 2000 as he pushed through several federal bills that further merged education with industrial production. President George W. Bush continued what his father and President Clinton began when he partnered with Senator Ted Kennedy to give us the federal education program No Child Left Behind.

The president's brother—Governor Jeb Bush of Florida—took advantage of the federal funds available from No Child Left Behind, and on June 5, 2006, he became the first governor in the nation to sign into law a bill that requires ninth-grade students to pick career majors. Several other states are not far behind and will soon join Florida in this radical manifestation of the Communist Manifesto.

Under Florida's new law, career exploration will begin as early as sixth grade. By ninth grade, students will need to declare their career majors. (Did you know what you wanted to do when you were in ninth grade?) Students will be encouraged to pick from careers that would place them either on a vocational track or on a college-bound track. With the assistance—or should we say, coercion—of school "career counselors," students will be channeled into the track the school in its wisdom thinks is best for the student. A ninth-grader who pursues a specific job such as auto mechanic may suddenly decide in his eleventh- or twelfth-grade year that he would like to go to college. Sadly, at this point a vocational-track student will be in a tough spot, since his course work is giving him vocational credits, not the college credits needed for a university.

There are some who think this is a good idea because not everyone is bound for college. I don't care if a student chooses to go to college or not. In many regards college is a waste of time and money unless you desire to be a doctor, lawyer, nurse, or other such professional. Several studies have revealed that many, if not most, of America's millionaires do not hold college degrees. A college degree is not needed for success, but a strong academic foundation from kindergarten through twelfth grade is essential for every student, regardless of whether he or she is vocation-bound, college-bound, or intends to be self-employed. Besides, the federal government is not qualified to project the supply and demand of the workforce even two years from now, much less ten years down the road.

Whether it is called ready-to-work, school-to-work, school-to-career, small learning communities or any other name, it still the tenth plank of the Communist Manifesto in action. And that shouldn't be put to work here in America!

8

WHY SCHOOL-TO-WORK DOESN'T WORK
LESSON 2

If you think school-to-work-style education reform is not occurring where you live, then you need to ask whether or not your state receives any federal education funds. If your state is *not* receiving federal dollars, this communist brand of education reform may not be taking place. But lest you be even slightly optimistic, I'll tell you plainly that I don't know of a single state that has rejected federal education funds—and the accompanying strings. That means it's happening right where you live. Whether through private grants, No Child Left Behind, or some other U.S. Department of Education and U.S. Department of Labor programs, states are rushing to comply with federal requirements so they can gorge themselves at Uncle Sam's money trough.

Florida, Minnesota, Illinois, Oregon, and Washington are further along in their implementation of school-to-work/ready-to-work/Small Learning Communities, but make no mistake. Every state in the union has school districts that are in some way weaving this reform package into their systems, thereby moving America down the road toward a centrally planned economy.

Yet abuses of people by this system abound. In Las Vegas, for example, Rene Tucker's daughter, Darcy, was pulled out of a geography class without her parents' consent in order to be given a computerized career assessment. Although Darcy wants to become a veterinarian, the computer held that she should be a bartender or waitress, and it spat out a list of courses she ought to take toward that end. Mrs. Tucker said, "We're Christians, and the school stepped on my toes as a parent. It is my job to direct my child's career path, and it would not be in her best interest to be a bartender." Given the gargantuan hospitality needs of the state, it might be in Nevada's best interest to turn Darcy into one of the minions of the gambling and entertainment industry, but that approach to career path development sounds more like it belongs in the 1960s Soviet Union than in 21st century America.

A few years ago I testified before the Kansas state senate along with Rene Tucker. We were joined by an economist from Hillsdale College to urge Kansas not to implement school-to-work in that state. But the anticipated tidal wave of federal funds was too much for the mere state of Kansas to resist, and on behalf of its people, the state legislature rejected common sense and freedom to imbibe the failed economic polices of communism.

In his classic book, *Brave New World*, Aldous Huxley wrote,

> To bring about the revolution we require...Enabling government managers to assign any given individual to his or her proper place in the social and economic hierarchy. Round pegs in square holes tend to have dangerous thoughts about the social system and to infect others with their discontents.

In other words, those who do not agree with the State's worldview or "standards" will not be encouraged to pursue positions of power or influence--either socially or economically.

The fact that so many Americans don't even know this communistic education reform is sweeping our nation is perilous. What is even more alarming is the ones who know it yet believe it is a good thing. Liberal Republicans and Democrats alike have succeeded in achieving the goals that Secular Humanists and Communists have long sought for America's children. And there, as they say, goes the future.

9

THE HUMANISTS' PRIME TARGET— EDUCATION IN THE CROSSHAIRS

M any years ago, Secular Humanists chose what area of American culture and influence they would infiltrate first with their seductive worldview. They agreed that if they could take over the nation's schools and make each one a school of humanism, they would eventually influence every American institution.

John J. Dunphy, a proud humanist, wrote in a contest-winning essay in the *Humanist* magazine:

> I am convinced that the battle for humankind's future must be waged and won in the public school classroom by teachers.... These teachers must embody the same selfless dedication of the most rabid fundamentalist preachers. For they will be ministers of another sort, utilizing a classroom instead of a pulpit to convey humanist values in whatever subject they teach, regardless of the education level—preschool, day care, or large state university. The classroom must and will become an arena of conflict between the old and the new: the rotting corpse of Christianity, together with all its adjacent evils and misery, and the new faith of humanism. Humanism will emerge triumphant. It must if the family of humankind is to survive.[13]

America's educational system became the main focus of America's humanists for obvious reasons. The educational system offered the opportunity to mold and shape the impressionable worldview of young students. Charles Francis Potter, in his 1930 book, *Humanism: A New Religion*, explains the strategy:

> Education is thus a most powerful ally of Humanism, and every American public school is a school of Humanism. What can the theistic Sunday schools, meeting for an hour once a week, and teaching only a fraction of the children, do to stem the tide of a five-day program of humanistic teaching?[14]

Similarly, Brooks Alexander argued for the schools' influence:

> In the ideological contest for cultural supremacy, public education is the prime target; it influences the most people in the most pervasive way at the most impressionable age. No other social institution has anything close to the same potential for mass indoctrination.

If you are still skeptical about the strategic targeting of America's educational system by liberal humanists, then consider the words of famed New Age author Marilyn Ferguson. For her book *The Aquarian Conspiracy,* Ferguson surveyed many followers of the New Age movement—also known as Cosmic Humanism—and she reports that "more were involved in education than in any other single category of work. They were teachers, administrators, policy makers, and educational psychologists."

In 1986, Paul C. Vitz conducted a study of America's schools and textbooks, funded by the National Institute of Education, part of the Department of Education. Vitz documented that the

Secular Humanist worldview dominated the nation's textbooks and that the Christian worldview was excluded. In his report Vitz explains the dramatic influence Secular Humanism is having on America's educational system:

> [A] very widespread secular and liberal mindset… pervades the leadership of education (and textbook publishing), and a secular and liberal bias is its inevitable consequence… Whether one calls it secular humanism, enlightenment universalism, skeptical modernism, or just plain permissive liberalism, the bottom line is that a very particular and narrow sectarian philosophy has taken control of American education.[15]

While Vitz acknowledges that many public school teachers possess traditional American values, he makes it very clear that the *leadership* of today's educational system is far less than traditional in their worldview—and they are the ones who oversee curriculum and textbook development:

> Given the overwhelming secular philosophies characterizing American education in the last fifty years, it is to be expected that leaders in education will differ markedly from the general American public in the area of basic moral values.[16]

American parents have been intimidated by the "experts"— the liberal educational elite—into being silent and leaving educational policy up to them. The specialists argue that they are the ones who have the training and experience to know what our children need. The undermining of parental authority is all too common among humanist educators, who see conservative

41

parents, their traditional values, and the Christian worldview as an obstacle to successful brainwashing of our children.

Every Gallup survey for many years has shown that the overwhelming majority of Americans believe in God. Why then do we allow a small minority—who not only deny God but teach moral relativism abhorrent to His character—to set educational policy for us? It's a cruel shot at the heart of our way of life.

GOD AND SCIENCE—
TOGETHER AGAIN

10

GOOD REASON TO BELIEVE GOD EXISTS

Most liberals build arguments for their beliefs on no foundation at all. They prefer instead to classify their opponents as non-intellectual, old-fashioned, or perhaps even just plain stupid. That way, liberals can insulate themselves from accountability to reason. Their ideas don't have to stand up to scrutiny from intellectually sound debate.

This is nowhere more true than when liberals talk about God. The rest of us make logical connections between what we see and reality. When you look at a beautiful painting, for instance, you assume a gifted artist painted it. As you marvel at the buildings in a skyline, you think an architect designed them. Anything that looks designed, we figure, must have had a designer.

For liberals, though, that logic applies only to relatively simple design projects like skyscrapers, classic paintings, dams (if approved by the EPA), airports, and computer software. But when a truly complex design presents itself—cell structure, DNA, ecosystems, or galaxies—naturalists somehow miss the starting point. The astounding design, order and complexity of the universe loudly proclaim a designer. And the greater the design, the greater the designer, right?

Yes, unless you're a liberal.

Historian and philosopher of science Stephen Meyer is clear on this point: "We have not yet encountered any good in principle reason to exclude design from science."[17]

World-famous statistician George Gallup also weighs in: "I could prove God statistically! Take the human body alone. The chance that all the functions of the individual would just happen is a statistical monstrosity!"[18]

With Gallup's observation in mind, let's note just a few examples of what he finds so compellingly logical about seeing design around us:

• The brain weighs just over three pounds but can process data with a sophistication that a room full of CPUs can't. Fifteen billion neurons keep your brain humming through more than 100,000 billion (10^{14}) electrical connections—more than all the connections in all the electrical appliances in the world.[19]

• In the fraction of a second it takes you to read one word on this page, your bone marrow produces over 100,000 red blood cells. [20]

• The human eye contains 130,000 light-sensitive rods and cones which generate photochemical reactions that convert light into electrical impulses. One billion of these impulses are transmitted to the brain every second.

• The ear is as much an acoustic marvel as the eye is an optic one. It can distinguish 15,000 different tones, and not only does the ear hear, but it also controls your body's equilibrium.

• Regarding the intricacy of a typical cell, D.G. Lindsay explains, "Within each tiny cell are power plants that generate energy; factories that produce foods essential for life; complex transportation systems that guide specific chemicals from one location to another; barricades that control the import and export of materials across the cell."[21]

• Even Bill Gates notes the remarkable nature of the DNA within each cell: "DNA is like a computer program, but far, far more advanced than any software we've ever created."[22] (Got that? DNA is the equivalent of a software program, and everyone knows a program *had to have a programmer*.)

So the next time you're intrigued by a good mystery story, sending an email through cyberspace, or cruising an interstate highway and want to think of these creations the way a liberal would, simply remind yourself that they all "just happened."

11

FOSSIL, FOSSIL, WHO'S GOT THE FOSSIL?

Many of our natural history museums are silent purveyors of liberal-think, so remember, the next time you visit one: Don't believe everything you see.

While you may come across magnificent assemblies of ancient dinosaur bones, if you observe something labeled as a "transitional fossil," consider it a red flag—because there is no such thing as a bona fide transitional fossil. Nevertheless, some museums have actually manufactured them in order to support the politically correct, humanistic worldview that says we and all other animal species came about through macro-evolution. Although a few have enough integrity to note that the display fossils are manmade, the disclaimer will likely be small and hard to find.

When I tell you that no fossil evidence supports the evolutionary concept that "simpler" species morphed over time into more complex animals, please understand that it is not just fringe religious nuts who make this assertion. Charles Darwin himself was among the first to puzzle over the lack of transitional fossils. Based on his theory, Darwin had expected to find countless animal relics to support the notion of gradual development of species. He was clearly perplexed by the lack of evidence:

> Why is not every geological formation and every stratum full of such intermediate links? Geology assuredly does not reveal any such finely graduated organic chain; and this is the most obvious and serious objection which can be urged against the theory.[23]

Darwin could suppose that there was simply more need for exploration since fossil hunting was in its infancy in the mid-1800s. But more than a century after Darwin published *Origin of Species*, Dr. Colin Patterson, an evolutionist with the British Museum of Natural History, wrote a book that did not include any pictures of transitional fossils. When one of his readers wrote to ask why Patterson had omitted pictures, the scientist responded honestly:

> I fully agree with your comments on the lack of direct illustration of evolutionary transitions in my book. If I knew of any, fossil or living, I would certainly have included them. You suggest that an artist should be used to visualize such transformations, but where would he get the information from? I could not, honestly, provide it, and if I were to leave it to artistic license, would that not mislead the reader?... As a paleontologist myself, I am much occupied with the philosophical problems of identifying ancestral forms in the fossil record. You say that I should at least "show a photo of the fossil from which each type of organism was derived." I will lay it on the line—there is not one such fossil for which one could make a watertight argument.[24]

You may well be surprised to hear these candid worries by evolutionists. The facts about transitional fossils are hard to come by. Often, "experts" have intentionally led people to believe what is simply not true. Consider, for example, all those alleged ape-man bones that were used to draw textbook pictures of humans developing from ape into man. Millions upon millions of school children have seen them over the past half-century. But note well the real truth about these deceptive images. Dr. Walter Brown in his book *In the Beginning* explains:

> It is now universally acknowledged that Piltdown man was a hoax, and yet it was in textbooks for over forty years.

> The only evidence for Nebraska man turned out to be a pig's tooth.

> Prior to 1978, the evidence for Ramapithecus consisted of a mere handful of teeth and jaw fragments. It is now known that these fragments were pieced together incorrectly by Louis Leakey in a form resembling part of the human jaw. Ramapithecus was just an ape.

> Eugene Dubois acknowledged forty years ago when he discovered Java "man" that it was probably just a large gibbon. Dubois also admitted that he had withheld parts of four other bones of apes, found in the same area, that supported that conclusion

> The fossils of Peking man are considered by many experts to be the remains of apes that were systematically decapitated and exploited for food by true man. Furthermore, Skull 1470, discovered by Richard Leakey, is more humanlike and yet older than Homo erectus (Java man and Peking man) and the Australopithecines. Since man cannot be older than his ancestors, something is obviously wrong....

> For about 100 years the world was led to believe that Neanderthal man was stooped and apelike. Recent studies show that this erroneous belief was based

upon some Neanderthal men who were crippled with arthritis and rickets. Neanderthal man, Heidelberg man, and Cro-Magnon man were completely human. Artists' depictions of them, especially of their fleshly portions, are often quite imaginative and are not supported by the evidence.

Furthermore, the techniques used to date these fossils are highly questionable.[25]

It is suspiciously ironic that when these various "discoveries" were unearthed, the liberal media turned it into big news. Yet when the discoveries were proven false and that they do not substantiate transitional evolution, the same media outlets either did not mention the new findings or did so on the "back page in small print."

A reasonable question becomes: If the fossil record does not show transitional forms or a species evolving from one animal into another, then what does it reveal? Historian Oswald Spengler offers the logical answer:

We find perfectly stable and unaltered forms preserving through long ages, forms that have not developed themselves on the fitness principle, but appear suddenly and at once in their definitive shape; that do not thereafter evolve towards better adaptation, but become rarer and finally disappear....[26]

That means macro-evolution (the Darwinian kind) never happened.

12

THE CHILLING TRUTH ABOUT GLOBAL WARMING
REALITY CHECK #1

Global warming is a hot issue, not because it's a real problem, but because many would like to scare you into thinking it is. Consider this report:

> Mayor Bloomberg yesterday compared the scourge of global warming to the threat of terrorism and the proliferation of weapons of mass destruction. Although it is a "long-term" fight, he said, reducing gas emissions may save the life of "everybody" on the planet, the same way that fighting terrorism and its proliferation saves lives in shorter terms.[27]

The New York mayor believes this even though more than 10,000 scientists don't. For example, Michael Griffin, head of NASA, has said he does not see global warming as a threat.

But what about all the disastrous consequences the alarmists say are already upon us? Let's see how many of their predictions have come true:

- Not so many years ago scientists predicted that the seas would rise from 20 to 40 feet because of global warming. On waves crashing against the base of the U.S. Capitol building, someone could launch boats from the bottom steps; one-third of Florida and large parts of Texas were projected to be under water. Now, however, estimates have been radically revised to a maximum water rise of several inches to just a few feet.[28]

- In the 1970s, scientists claimed aerosols were a leading cause of harm to the environment, but a recent report now shows that aerosols eventually have a cooling effect on global temperatures which helps cancel out the warming effect of CO_2.[29]

- In the 1920s, scientists warned of a fast approaching glacial age, but in the 1930s, they reversed themselves and predicted serious global warming. By 1972, *Time* magazine cited numerous scientific reports warning of runaway glaciation, and in 1975, *Newsweek* reported overwhelming scientific evidence that "proved" an approaching ice age. Some even advanced ideas to melt the artic ice cap in an effort to forestall the coming ice age.[30]

- In 1976, the U.S. government released a study affirming that the earth is heading into a mini-ice age. Now, however, the doomsday prediction of an imminent ice age has been replaced with the warning of a global warming disaster. In less than a century, environmental science has reversed itself on this issue no less than three times![31]

We could fill pages with unfulfilled end-of-the-world-as-we-know-it scenarios, but these few should be enough to reveal the undependable predictions of the global warming doomsayers.

Global warming proponents base their belief on the alleged fact that temperatures are rising. But are they? Here are the facts:

- The temperature fell throughout the 1920s, rose during the 1930s, fell again during the 1960s, and has been rising since the 1980s, according to one study.[32]

- Professor Bob Carter, a geologist at James Cook University, Queensland, Australia, says the global warming theory is neither environmental nor scientific, but rather, "a self-created political fiasco." Carter explains that "climate changes occur naturally all the time, partly in predictable cycles and partly in unpredictable cycles."[33]

- According to Robert Essenhigh, professor of energy conservation at Ohio State University, the ice sheets at the poles have been melting since the early 1900s, and the earth's warming had begun about the middle 1600s.[34]

Some studies show that the earth's temperature has risen and others indicate it has fallen. Why can't experts agree on the temperature? For starters, the earth's temperatures are taken in two different ways, and one method is not as reliable as the other. Dr. S. Fred Singer, an atmospheric physicist at George Mason University, explains:

You have to be very careful with the surface record. It is taken with thermometers that are mostly located in or near cities. And as cities expand, they get warmer. And therefore they affect the readings. And it's very difficult to eliminate this—what's called the urban heat island effect. So I personally prefer to trust in weather satellites… And if you look through the summary [of the United Nation's Intergovernmental Panel on Climate Change (IPCC)], you will find no mention of the fact that the weather satellite observations of the last twenty years show no global warming. In fact, a slight cooling. In fact, you will not even find satellites mentioned in the summary. These are the only global observations we have. They are the best observations we have. They cover the whole globe. They don't cover the oceans very well, which is 70% of the globe. So you see, the [U.N.] summary uses data selectively, or at least it suppresses data that are inconvenient, that disagree with the paradigm with what they're trying to prove."[35]

But regardless of temperature issues, we know the rise in sea level threatens much of civilization, don't we? That would be "No." In the April 16, 2007, issue of *Newsweek International,* Richard S. Lindzen of the Massachusetts Institute of Technology published an article, "Why So Gloomy," in which he notes:

The ill effects of warming are overblown. Sea levels, for example, have been increasing since the end of the last ice age. When you look at recent centuries in perspective, ignoring short-term fluctuations, the rate of sea-level rise has been relatively uniform (less than a couple of millimeters a year). There's even some evidence that the rate was higher in the fist half of the twentieth century than in the second half. Overall, the risk of sea-level rise from global warming is less at almost any given location than that from other causes, such as tectonic motions of the earth's surface. There is no compelling evidence that the warming trend we've seen will amount to anything close to catastrophe.[36]

Not exactly a compelling reason to start building another ark.

13

THE CHILLING TRUTH ABOUT GLOBAL WARMING
REALITY CHECK #2

I f you're beginning to get the idea that global warming as we know it is a myth, congratulations. But have you stopped to wonder who's behind all this myth-mongering? There are three primary players:

1. Cosmic Humanists (New Agers). These folks believe in pantheism, that all is god and god is all and Mother Earth should be worshipped. Radical environmentalists and animal rights extremists—many of whom come from this group—place more value on the earth and animals than on humans.

2. Globalists and socialists. Globalists—many of whom haunt the United Nations—intend to erode America's national sovereignty and create a one-world government. The United Nations' global warming treaty—the Kyoto Protocol—would seriously damage America's free enterprise system and yet it does not even apply to some of the world's biggest polluters, such as China and India.

3. Scientists and think-tanks. You've heard the old saying, "follow the money"? When you follow the trail behind the GW myth, it leads you to "scientists" who are willing to say anything to keep government grant money flowing their way. Some studies place U.S. government spending on climate change as high as $4 billion per year. Tom DeWeese, president of the American Policy Center, explains how this works in an article entitled "Fanatics, Heretics and the Truth about Global Warming":

Simply put, scientists know where the grants will come from to pay their salaries. Dr. Patrick Michaels, a leading opponent to the global warming scaremongers, calls it the federal/science paradigm. He describes it this way: Tax $ = Grants = Positive Feedback Loop to Get more Grants.

Says Dr. Michaels, "What worker bee scientist is going to write a proposal saying that global warming is exaggerated and he doesn't need the money? Certainly no one wanting advancement in the agency! There is no alternative to this process when paradigms compete with each other for finite funding." The only ones who can openly oppose the party line of the day are those who don't need the grants or who have some other source of funding. There aren't many.[37]

DeWeese goes on to detail why there is so much money in the global warming racket:

The money is in global warming because it's being pushed by a political agenda that wants power. They want power in Washington, power on the international stage, power over economic development, power over international monetary decisions, and power over energy. In short, power over the motor world. It's driven by literally thousands of large and small non-governmental organizations (NGOs) sanctioned by the United Nations, and implemented by a horde of bureaucrats, university academics and an ignorant but pliable news media.[38]

The GW crowd has told us that manmade carbon dioxide is the reason for the supposed rise in global temperatures. However, Robert Essenhigh, professor of energy conservation at Ohio State University, gives the lie to their claim:

> The two principal thermal-absorbing and thermal-emitting compounds in the atmosphere are water and carbon dioxide. However—and this point is continually missed—the ratio of water to carbon dioxide is something like 30-to-1 as an average value. At the top it is something like 100-to-1. This means that the carbon dioxide is simply 'noise' in the water concentration, and anything carbon dioxide could do, water has already done. So, if the carbon dioxide is increasing, is it the carbon dioxide driving the temperature or is the rising temperature driving up the carbon dioxide? In other words, *the carbon dioxide issue is irrelevant to the debate over global warming.*[39] [emphasis mine]

As I've pointed out, the reality is that the temperature of the earth goes up and down in cycles. And the cause of the up-cycle is the sun. Perhaps we need legislation to control our big solar neighbor in the sky? You might note, too, that—according to *Access to Energy*—Mars, Jupiter, and Pluto are also warming up. It's doubtful U. S. companies have caused that.

Dr. Sallie Baliunas, an astrophysicist who serves as senior scientist at the George C. Marshall Institute in Washington D.C. and who chairs the Institute's Science Advisory Board, gave a lecture on February 12, 2008, at the University of Texas entitled, "Warming Up to the Truth: The Real Story about Climate Change." Dr. Baliunas says the warming and cooling of the earth is more related to solar variability than it is carbon dioxide in the atmosphere. In other words, the increase and decrease in *solar output* has led to the cyclical warming and cooling of the earth.[40]

So if you think the variation of temperature by a degree or two in one way or another is worthy of destroying America, free enterprise, and our national sovereignty, then hop on the bandwagon. Otherwise, keep your cool, and don't buy the nonsense.

PLAYING BY
WHOSE RULES?

14

WHO SAYS YOU CAN'T LEGISLATE MORALITY?

Many people who consider themselves intellectually sophisticated claim no one should ever "legislate morality" and any who would try to are violating the "separation of church and state." I dare say, "You can't legislate morality" is one of the most-quoted phrases of liberals when they oppose a piece of legislation but have a weak argument against its passage. Unfortunately, many Christians have bought this silly line of reasoning without thinking about it. The reality is that liberals have gotten very good at legislating *their* morality.

All laws impose someone's morality. Those of us who desire to see partial-birth abortion outlawed are attempting to bring our Biblical morality and worldview to bear on the issue. Those who oppose banning the procedure desire to maintain a morality based on their humanistic, relativistic worldview. The truth is, our laws legislate morality every day. The question is not *whether* morality can be legislated but, rather, *whose* morality will be legislated.

Laws against murder, rape, stealing, child pornography, or kidnapping are all laws that legislate morality. Such laws call for people not to do these hurtful things. But what about those who argue, "Just because you legislate morality doesn't mean people will obey the law"? Their statement is true, of course, but just because not everyone obeys the law does not mean we should eliminate the law. If perfect obedience were the measure of the rightness of a law, we would have no laws at all. Everyone would just do what is right in his or her own eyes.

Sometimes there's another argument forthcoming: "You cannot change the heart with legislation." But the changing of a person's heart is not the foremost goal of legislating morality. Nonetheless, statistics show that the overwhelming majority of people in America obey laws even when they are not being watched. Most voluntarily pay their taxes, register for the Selective Service at age 18, and drive the speed limit. As long as the law caused that individual to control his immoral impulses for fear of retribution, then the law has done its job.

Even so, there is historical evidence that, over time, laws *can* change people's hearts. Take slavery, for instance. At the time slavery was outlawed, many people still thought they should be allowed to enslave other individuals based on the color of their skin. Today, however, you would be hard-pressed to find someone in America who genuinely thinks slavery is morally acceptable. Over time, the law has caused most people to think of slavery as immoral. Today, Americans obey anti-slavery laws not for fear of retribution but out of a heart's desire to respect their fellow man's right to freedom—regardless of his skin color.

Unfortunately, such a process can also work against improvements in morality. In 1960, very few Americans would have agreed that abortion, the killing of an unborn child, is morally acceptable. It was certainly something most pregnant mothers would not do, and neither the father nor mother of a pregnant girl would encourage her to get an abortion. Even the unmarried father of an unborn baby was less likely to encourage his girlfriend to murder the child they had conceived together. But because the U.S. Supreme Court—the highest judicial authority in our land—has ruled that abortion is legal, many Americans have come to consider abortion morally acceptable. The Court's position on the issue has had a powerful—and negative—impact on the morals of millions, because most people equate what the law says with what is right and moral. What a disaster when the government encourages immorality!

Why did the Founders decide that America's laws were to be based on God's laws? Because they not only understood that God's way is the best way, regardless of culture or religion, but they also knew God's moral law is written on the hearts of all people. In *Original Intent*, David Barton writes, "The Founders believed the Bible to be the perfect example of moral legislation and the source of what they called, 'the moral law.' For nearly 150 years, the courts agreed and relied on this moral law as the basis for our civil laws."[41]

Scripture offers numerous verses that call us to promote righteousness, which is exactly what "legislating morality" does:

- Blessed are those who hunger and thirst for righteousness, because they will be filled. (Matthew 5:6)

- Righteousness exalts a nation, but sin is a disgrace to any people. (Proverbs 14:34)

- A city is built up by the blessing of the upright, but it is torn down by the mouth of the wicked. (Proverbs 11:11)

- When the righteous flourish, the people rejoice, but when the wicked rule, people groan. (Proverbs 29:2)

Yes, we can—and should—legislate morality. Most importantly, Christians must be involved in the process if we desire to promote righteousness and be salt and light in a dark world. After all, if God, the Ultimate Law-giver, created government, shouldn't His people use the legislative process to promote His morality? The purveyors of religion-without-God have already been doing that. It's time we shift the momentum back toward the real truth and nothing but the truth.

15

RELIGION AND LAW
GO HAND IN HAND

One great goal of the liberal rewrite of American history is to hard-sell the deception that religion and law are anathema to each another. If liberals repeat often enough the debased notion that America's Founders were sophisticated humanists (like them), then liberals have a good chance of shaming the rest of us into accepting that our God-fearing sensibilities have no place in the public square.

Fortunately, it's very hard to rewrite writings that have been in print for more than two centuries. In fact, it's actually kind of fun to see the havoc the real story of our early thinkers plays with today's liberal minds. Take, for instance, America's most respected legal scholar at the time of the Founders, William Blackstone, who wrote pointedly about the connection between religion and law:

> Man, considered as a creature, must necessarily be subject to the law of his creator, for he is entirely a dependent being.... And consequently, as man depends absolutely upon his maker for everything, it is necessary that he should in all points conform to his maker's will. This will of his maker is called the law of nature.... This law of nature, being coeval with mankind and dictated by God himself, is of course superior in obligation to all other. It is binding over all the globe, in all countries, and at all times; no human laws are of any validity, if contrary to this; and such of them as are valid derive all

their force, and all their authority, mediately or immediately, from this original.[42]

Blackstone, of course, was not alone in his views. James Wilson, a signer of the Constitution and one of our original Supreme Court justices, wrote several of America's early legal commentaries, and this is what he had to say about the relationship between law and religion:

> Human law must rest its authority ultimately upon the authority of that law which is Divine... Far from being rivals or enemies, religion and law are twin sisters, friends, and mutual assistants. Indeed, these two sciences run into each other. The Divine law...forms an essential part of both.[43]

George Washington also understood that without religious convictions—without a religious worldview that acknowledges absolute moral truth, good and evil, right and wrong, justice and injustice—there is no foundation for morality and peace. In his "Farewell Address," President Washington posed this pointed question: "Let it be simply asked, 'Where is the security for life, for reputation, and for property, if the sense of religious obligation desert?'"[44] He also answered it:

> Let us with caution indulge the supposition that morality can be maintained without religion. Whatever may be conceded to the influence of refined education on minds...reason and experience both forbid us to expect that national morality can prevail in exclusion of religious principle.[45]

Humanistic liberals believe in only the natural world. As they see it, this world occurred by accident, for no purpose, and there is no supernatural God or anything else like Him behind it all. This worldview allows liberals to base law on their own reasoning, their own desires, and their own man-centered understanding of life. It gives them an "out" against being bound by or accountable to the God who created natural and divine laws.

But they are not willing to face the necessary conclusion derived from their worldview. It is reasonable to think that without an eternal, all-knowing, holy God, there can be no law that is just, fair, and coherent. Apart from God, man is left with only himself. Liberals ignore that troublesome nature within us that tends toward evil.

If all that exists is the natural world, then the survival of the fittest and "might makes right" are the only real laws. Only a self-absorbed humanist can believe that man could be the source of laws that protect the righteous, punish the wicked, secure peace, and seek justice for all. But we have seen the consequences of such a worldview as lived out by Hitler, Stalin, Mussolini, and other humanist models of absolute power in action.

If all that exists is the natural world, then it does not matter what the laws are. Why? Because there is no one to judge or punish us for breaking or keeping the laws of nature. Laws make sense only if they were put in place by a supernatural source, as a reflection of our Creator's goodness, mercy, holiness, and love of justice.

This is what sets man apart from the animals. We are created in God's image and live by the moral law, or Ten Commandments, etched on our minds and hearts. And inscribed, by the way, on our Supreme Court building.

16

OUR FOUNDERS INTENDED RELIGION SHOULD BE KEPT AWAY FROM PUBLIC LIFE.
NOT.

I t is fashionably progressive (i.e., liberal) to portray the Founding Fathers as rationalistic, humanistic, or deistic thinkers
dedicated to purely "objective" intellectual pursuits unen-
cumbered by religion or matters of faith. As such, elitists argue,
the Founders certainly would endorse the liberal contention that
religion and the accompanying moral strictures have "no place in
the public square."

If the liberals' contention were true, you might expect to find
in the writings of the Founders such statements as this:

> We affirm that moral values derive their source
> from human experiences. Ethics is autonomous and
> situational, needing no theological or ideological sanc-
> tion. Ethics stems from human need and interest. To
> deny this distorts the whole basis of life. Human life has
> meaning because we create and develop our futures.

And perhaps you might also assume they would say things
such as:

> Individuals should be encouraged to realize their
> own creative talents and desires. We reject all religious,
> ideological, or moral codes that denigrate the individu-
> al, suppress freedom....

Sounds like solid, humanistic thinking, doesn't it? The kind you would expect from humanistic, rationalistic thinkers, if that's what our Founders were like. These statements, however, come not from any document signed by freedom-loving souls like Thomas Jefferson, John Hancock, or Benjamin Franklin. No, the above quotations come from a document, signed by many avowed socialists and communists, called the *Humanist Manifesto II*.

However, if you want to get a clear picture of what sort of principles America was founded upon, you will want to pay attention to writings like this one from John Jay, the first chief justice of the U.S. Supreme Court:

> Providence has given to our people the choice of their rulers, and it is the duty—as well as the privilege and interest—of our Christian nation to select and prefer Christians for their rulers.[46]

Or check in with the "Northwest Ordinance." Although few people today know much about this pivotal document, it was nevertheless crucial in the early days of the American republic. The ordinance presented guidelines for how a territory could become a state, and among its many provisions is this telling statement from Article III:

> Religion, morality, and knowledge, *being necessary to good government* and the happiness of mankind, schools and the means of education shall forever be encouraged. [emphasis mine]

Elitists on the Supreme Court, as well as in other, lesser jurisdictions, seem to have missed the "forever" part of that message. As it turns out, "forever" has only lasted until about halfway through the twentieth century. Starting in 1947 and continuing through specific rulings in 1962, 1963, 1980, and 2000, religion and morality have been surgically removed from our governmental enterprises, with the most notable evisceration occurring in our nation's public schools. Now, children can't pray, courthouses can't set up manger scenes, state seals have had crosses forcibly removed from the design, and generally, it must be assumed that we no longer consider religion, morality, and such knowledge "necessary to good government."

If the truth be told, keeping religion and morality out of the public arena wasn't the Founders' idea. That calling has been taken up—and the Founders' authority usurped—by the modern United States Supreme Court and its liberal backers.

17

THE AMERICAN CIVIL LIBERTIES UNION (ACLU)
AND
AMERICA'S FUNDAMENTAL FREEDOMS

"The most effective humanist organization for destroying the laws, morals, and traditional rights of
Americans has been the ACLU. Founded in 1920,
it is the legal arm of the humanist movement...."[47]

Why be subtle? Tim LaHaye and David Noebel, in their inci-
sive exposé *Mind Siege*, hit the nail on the head.

The naming of the American Civil *Liberties* Union was pure
marketing genius, but the history of the organization shouts loudly about what a lie it is to suggest that the group's goals have anything to do with preserving American freedoms as envisioned by
our Founders. The ACLU has founders of its own whose agenda
is frightening to America's well-being and whose résumés leave
no doubt what principles they hold dear:

- John Dewey, often called the "father of modern education," is a signer of *Humanist Manifesto I*, was a board
  member of the American Humanist Association, and
  was an early supporter of the socialist League for Industrial Democracy.

- William Z. Foster once led the United States Communist Party.

- Roger Baldwin, the first head of the ACLU, set up
  the organization's original office in New York in space

shared with the Communist Party's *New Masses* tabloid. Baldwin "also launched the Mutual Aid Society to offer financial help to leftist intellectuals, trade unionists, and the radical fringe,"[48] and he created the International Committee for Political Prisoners "to provide counsel and support to anarchist and communist subversives who had been deported for their criminal activities."[49]

At one time, an evidently far wiser and discerning U.S. Congress than we have today even smelled the rat behind the patriotic-sounding name. On January 17, 1931, the U.S. House of Representatives special committee investigating communist activities in the United States reported:

> The American Civil Liberties Union is closely affiliated with the communist movement in the United States, and fully 90 percent of its efforts are on behalf of communists who have come into conflict with the law. It claims to stand for free speech, free press, and free assembly, but it is quite apparent that the main function of the ACLU is to attempt to protect the communists in their advocacy of force and violence to overthrow the Government, replacing the American flag by a red flag and erecting a Soviet Government in place of the republican form of government guaranteed to each state by the Federal Constitution.

As I have said, why be subtle? Congress saw no need. Yet the truth behind the ACLU is lost on virtually every major media player and many elected officials. Or more ominously, perhaps they know the truth about the ACLU, and they're happy to reinforce the lie to the general public.

While we're on a roll with not being subtle, we might as well let Baldwin himself add his comment on the truth behind the façade he founded:

> We want to look like patriots in everything we do. We want to get a lot of flags, talk a great deal about the Constitution and what our forefathers wanted to make of this country and how we are the fellows that really stand for the spirit of our institutions.[50]

But Baldwin's bottom-most line? "I wanted what the Communists wanted, and I traveled the United Front road to get it."[51]

To invoke a helpful cliché, "Need I say more?"

18

GETTING TAKEN ON THE
SEPARATION OF CHURCH AND STATE

Many Americans think the term "separation of church and state" is taken straight from the U.S. Constitution, but they are, in fact, the ones who have been "taken." The "separation" phrase was written by Thomas Jefferson, although not in the context in which it has come to be used since the middle of the twentieth century.

The term "separation of church and state" originated in a letter written by Thomas Jefferson on New Year's Day 1802 to a Baptist denominational group. The Danbury Baptist Association feared the fledgling federal government might establish some form of state church that would make life difficult for those not within the boundaries of whichever denomination became the official religion. Jefferson explained why the clergymen had nothing to fear:

> Believing with you that religion is a matter which lies solely between man and his God, that he owes account to none other for faith or his worship, that the legislative powers of government reach actions only, and not opinions, I contemplate with solemn reverence that act of the whole American people which declared that their legislature should "make no law respecting an establishment of religion, or prohibiting the free exercise," thus building a wall of separation of Church and State.[52]

The separation was intended not to keep the church from

intervening in government but to keep the government from in-terfering with the church. For more than a century, Jefferson's clear intent was honored, but in 1947 the U.S. Supreme Court hi-jacked the phrase "separation of church and state," ripped it from its historical context, and created a new meaning, completely op-posed to its original intent.

The original draft of the First Amendment to the Constitu-tion was introduced in the Senate on September 3, 1789, and stated, "Congress shall not make any law establishing any reli-gious denomination." The second version said, "Congress shall make no law establishing any particular denomination." The third version was similar, declaring, "Congress shall make no law es-tablishing any particular denomination in preference to another." But the final version, passed later that same day, became the First Amendment that is still part of our Constitution: "Congress shall make no law establishing religion or prohibiting the free exercise thereof."[53]

Other sources also reinforce the perspective that the intent of our Founders was not to restrict religion. In fact, the Found-ers required any territory applying for statehood to show respect for religious sensibilities as directed by the Northwest Ordinance, which governed applications for states to join the Union.[54]

Nineteenth-century U.S. Supreme Court Justice Joseph Story weighed in on the meaning of the First Amendment: "The whole power over the subject of religion is left exclusively to the State governments to be acted upon according to their own sense of justice and the State constitutions."[55] Story believed the First Amendment was not written to suppress Christianity but to keep Christian denominations from competing with each other to become the official national religion. As Story points out, the

Founders did not want anyone—even if their beliefs were contrary to Christianity—to be persecuted for their religious beliefs or convictions:

> The real object of the First Amendment was not to countenance, much less to advance, Mahomedism [Islam], or Judaism, or infidelity, by prostrating Christianity; but to exclude all rivalry among Christian sects, and to prevent any national ecclesiastical establishment, which should give to a hierarchy the exclusive patronage of the national government. It thus cut off the means of religious persecution (the vice and pest of former ages), and of the subversion of the rights of conscience in matters of religion which had been trampled upon almost from the days of the Apostles to the present age…. An attempt to level all religions and to make it a matter of state policy to hold all in utter indifference would have created universal disapproval, if not universal indignation.[56]

The Founding Fathers would be appalled that judges have used the Constitution as a weapon to strip the states of their God-given rights. In a clarion summary statement, Gouverneur Morris, a Founder who wrote the first draft of the Constitution, declares that the sole purpose of the Constitution is to protect freedom and liberty, not to justify tyranny: "The Constitution is not an instrument for government to restrain people, it is an instrument for the people to restrain the government—lest it come to dominate our lives and interests."[57]

Of the delegates that attended the Constitutional Convention in Philadelphia in 1787, only 39 out of 55 would sign the

Constitution. Many who would not refused because they believed the Constitution at that point did not contain the safeguards needed to keep the central government in check. To break the stalemate, the first ten amendments to the Constitution—the Bill of Rights—were created to be handcuffs on the central government, limiting its power and protecting the rights of the states

As always, history makes clear who's been duped by common myths.

19

GOD'S PLAN FOR GOOD GOVERNMENT

L iberals love it when conservatives fight among themselves—especially when the battle centers around
whether or not America is truly based on a Biblical foundation and God's providential work. In case you're blissfully
ignorant about the controversy, let me explain.

A nationally known pastor (whom I appreciate and agree
with most of the time) has actually written that the founding of
America was a sin:

> Over the past several centuries, people have mis-
> takenly linked democracy and political freedom to
> Christianity. That's why many contemporary evangeli-
> cals believe the American Revolution was completely
> justified, both politically and scripturally. They follow
> the arguments of the Declaration of Independence,
> which declares that life, liberty, and the pursuit of hap-
> piness are divinely endowed rights.
>
> Therefore those believers say such rights are part
> of a Christian worldview, worth attaining and defending
> at all cost including military insurrection at times. But
> such a position is contrary to the clear teachings and
> commands of Romans 13:1-7. So the United States was
> actually born out of a violation of New Testament prin-
> ciples, and any blessings God has bestowed on America
> have come in spite of that disobedience by the Found-
> ing Fathers.[58]

When you combine a lack of knowledge about the American Revolution with a false interpretation of Romans 13, you end up with good conservative Christians adding to the misinformation about our Founders and believing that America was *not* established under God but by an un-Christian rebellion. My friend and regular Worldview Weekend speaker David Barton has written a paper entitled "Was the American Revolution a Biblically Justified Act?" in which he notes:

> The Presbyterians, Lutherans, Baptists, Congregationalists, and most other Christian denominations during the American Revolution believed that Romans 13 meant they were not to overthrow government as an institution and live in anarchy. This passage does not mean they had to submit to every civil law. Note that in Hebrews 11, a number of those who made the cut in the "Faith Hall of Fame" as heroes of the faith were guilty of civil disobedience—including Daniel, the three Hebrew Children, the Hebrew Midwives, Moses, etc....
>
> If the Founding Fathers had removed themselves from underneath the authority of Great Britain because they were choosing anarchy over an established government, then that would be a violation of Romans 13. Although Romans 13 is not an endorsement of every government, it is a description of what God says is the proper role of civil government.[59]

In Scripture, God initiates several realms of authority in human governance: family, church, and state. These reflect the normal pattern of social interaction, and civilizations throughout history have reproduced these in some form. Simply because the presence of these institutions is normative, however, we should not expect every instance of them to be acceptable.

Fathers are the God-ordained head of the family, but those who abuse their children and wives deserve to be removed from their positions of authority. Few people disagree that a pastor or elder should be removed from leadership in the church—his God-ordained position of authority—if the leader is guilty of grave moral and ethical failures. And, as with church and family rule, God does not necessarily endorse every leader or every civil government that comes along.

For eleven years, our Founders petitioned the king of Great Britain to cease his unlawful, unBiblical actions against the colonials. Although the monarch ignored their grievances, they remained under his authority until he sent 25,000 troops into the colonies for the purpose of seizing property, invading homes, and imprisoning people without trials. The king's actions violated his own British common law, the English Bill of Rights, and the centuries-old Magna Carta.

Once King George III started down the path of violent suppression, the Founders announced their intent to separate from Great Britain. They wrote at length that they were involved in self-defense, which they rightly believed was Biblically acceptable. British troops fired the first shot in every confrontation leading up to the Revolutionary War—the Massacre of 1770, the bombing of Boston in 1774, and the Lexington and Concord engagements of 1775.

Unless you are a thoroughgoing pacifist, there is no basis for saying the Founders sinned in defending themselves against King George's troops and their terrorist tactics against the colonists. The Founders' fight was not a "military insurrection." Our early leaders took seriously their standing before God and believed He could bless a war of defense but not a war of offense. They fought to protect their own lives and those of their family and friends.

Many Christians get queasy over the subject of "civil disobedience" and invoke Romans 13 to avoid the responsibility of standing up to a deviant government. While I agree it is crucial that Christians pursue civil disobedience only when obeying government requires us to disobey God, Scripture offers clear direction on when such action is acceptable.

The Founding Fathers did not violate New Testament principles when they instituted American independence, and it is critical that we close ranks on this fundamental issue. Our nation was founded under God's guiding hand—not in *spite* of it. Whether or not we continue in the godly heritage of the first Americans is a vital concern, but it's one that should be debated between "us" and "them," not between "us" and "us."

20

WHY THE TEN COMMANDMENTS
STILL MATTER

Afailure to grasp the significance of the Bible in our society is common to religious citizens as well as non-
religious. Explaining why this shift in understanding
has occurred, George Barna states that Christian institutions
have failed to present a compelling case for Bible-based moral
truth:

> Most people do not believe there is any source of ab-
> solute moral truth. Even [self-professing] born-again
> individuals are abandoning the notion of law based on
> scriptural principles.[60]

The result of our misunderstanding is a downward spiral
into lawlessness and disorder. The deterioration of America's freedoms will continue because we now lack the key component to
sustain such freedom and liberties—knowledge and understanding of Biblical truths. In his book, *Original Intent*, David Barton
expands on this reality:

> The Founders understood that Biblical values formed
> the basis of the republic and that the republic would
> be destroyed if the people's knowledge of those values
> should ever be lost.... Understanding the foundation of
> the American republic is a vital key toward protecting it.
> Therefore, in analyzing public policy remember to ask,
> "Is this act consistent with our form of government?"

and support or oppose the policy on that basis.[61]

The battle to display the Ten Commandments in America's public buildings, for example, is not just a religious battle but a battle to maintain the very foundation of America's form of government. Without the moral law and without a Christian worldview, there is no foundation for America's constitutional republic. To separate the Biblical worldview from our republican form of government means that we abolish the form of government given to us by the Founders. Clearly, that is the goal of such groups as the ACLU, Americans United for the Separation of Church and State, and numerous socialistic, humanist organizations (supported by most major media outlets and usually the Democratic party as well).

While we're challenging popular but misguided notions, we might as well also mention that no less an influence in early America than Benjamin Rush even believed the Bible should be a textbook in America's schools. He considered Christianity the only worldview consistent with perpetuating our form of government:

> We profess to be republicans, and yet we neglect the only means of establishing and perpetuating our republican forms of government; that is, the universal education of our youth in the principles of Christianity by means of the Bible. For this Divine Book, above all others, favors that equality among mankind, that respect for just laws, and those sober and frugal virtues which constitute the soul of republicanism.[62]

In a similar vein, Noah Webster wrote a textbook entitled *History of the United States* in which he explained:

The brief exposition of the Constitution of the United States will unfold to young persons the principles of republican government; and it is the sincere desire of the writer that our citizens should early understand that the genuine source of correct republican principles is the Bible, particularly the New Testament or the Christian religion.[63]

Dr. Jedidiah Morse warned about the possibility of allowing this foundation to be undermined: "Whenever the pillars of Christianity shall be overthrown, our present republican forms of government, and all the blessings which flow from them, must fall with them."[64] The Founders cautioned repeatedly that we could not expect God's blessing or protection—and could very well face His wrath (how un-humanistic is that!)—if we make a practice of violating His principles.

George Mason, the Father of the Bill of Rights, speaking at the Constitutional Convention, declared: "As nations cannot be rewarded or punished in the next world, so they must be in this. By an inevitable chain of causes and effects, Providence punishes national sins by national calamities."[65]

A final note about public policy will help make clear why liberals are happy with the America-is-a-democracy lie: A democracy opens wide the door to fiscal policy that breeds redistribution schemes and dependency of the people on government. This dismal potential has been recognized for years. In 1787 (about the time our original 13 states adopted the Constitution) it is said that Alexander Tyler, a Scottish history professor at the University of Edinburgh, had this to say about "The Fall of The Athenian Republic" some 2,000 years prior:

A democracy is always temporary in nature; it simply cannot exist as a permanent form of government. A democracy will continue to exist up until the time that voters discover that they can vote themselves generous gifts from the public treasury. From that moment on, the majority always votes for the candidates who promise the most benefits from the public treasury, with the result that every democracy will finally collapse due to loose fiscal policy, (which is) always followed by a dictatorship.[66]

The average life span of the world's great civilizations has been about 200 years. During those 200 years, these nations progressed through the following sequence:

- From bondage to spiritual faith; from spiritual faith to great courage;

- From courage to liberty; from liberty to abundance;

- From abundance to complacency; from complacency to apathy;

- From apathy to dependence; from dependence back into bondage.[67]

America would appear to be somewhere between the apathy and dependence phase, which means bondage is right around the corner unless we wake up to the needed changes. Regardless of what any majority of Americans may want, every law, every piece of legislation, and all public policy must be consistent with the teachings of the Bible, or we are not operating under the rules of a constitutional republic. The basis of our freedom lies not in the whims of the majority, but in holding the potentially deviant will of the people in check. That is done by measuring our national will against Christian Scripture as the unchanging standard, and measuring whether we are being just or unjust, good or evil, right or wrong. .

21

PREYING ON THE NATIONAL FLOCK—
LAWYERS IN JUDGES' CLOTHING

Over the past few years, the U.S. Supreme Court has variously told American high school students they're not allowed to pray before a football game, denied states the right to outlaw homosexual sex, prohibited the display of the Ten Commandments on public property if it is for the purpose of acknowledging God, and permitted governments to confiscate private lands and give them to a more favored private entity.

Perhaps this is why U.S. Supreme Court Justice Antonin Scalia recently disdained certain foolish and dangerous rulings by federal judges—including his own colleagues on the Supreme Court. Scalia warns, "Anyone who thinks the country's most prominent lawyers reflect the views of the people needs a reality check." He proclaimed that "Joe Sixpack" is just as qualified as the average judge to make rulings in regard to abortion or gay marriage.

Bravo, Judge Scalia!

I fully agree that most Americans are more likely to render just and moral decisions than many a contemporary judge. After all, in most cases (so to speak), what is a judge other than a lawyer in a black robe?

Before you think I'm about to do nothing but bash lawyers, I'll acknowledge there are some outstanding attorneys in America. A few of the best, I know quite well: Steve Crampton, lead attorney for the American Center for Law and Policy, and David

Limbaugh, nationally syndicated columnist, best-selling author and regular Worldview Weekend speaker. But for the rest of this article, I'm going leave the bashing to several respectable attorneys. I hope you're shaken by the potential disaster we face as a nation because of the presence of too many lawyers in high places.

Lino Graglia, professor of constitutional law at the University of Texas School of Law, provides some expert insight into what goes into the making of a lawyer:

> The study and practice of law has many advantages, including the acquisition of great skill in the manipulation of words, but few would recommend it as a means of inculcating habits of ethical fastidiousness or devotion to candor. No person knowledgeable as to the making of lawyers or the practice of law can possibly believe that it is from among lawyers that we should select our ethical leaders or that to the lawyers selected we may safely grant governmental authority.

Countless surveys have made it axiomatic that most Americans believe lawyers are among the most unethical people in America. And lawyers' malignant behavior shows up in sad statistics about how they view themselves. C. Patrick Schiltz in *Notre Dame Magazine* points out:

> Lawyers suffer from depression, anxiety, hostility, paranoia, social alienation and isolation, obsessive-compulsiveness, and interpersonal sensitivity at alarming rates. For example, research affiliated with Johns Hopkins University found statistically significant elevations of major depressive disorder (AMDD) in only three of

104 occupations: lawyers, pre-kindergarten and special education teachers, and secretaries. Lawyers topped the list.... Lawyers also suffer from alcoholism and use illegal drugs at rates far higher than non-lawyers.... Not surprisingly, a preliminary study indicates that lawyers commit suicide and think about committing suicide more than non-lawyers.[68]

I believe the source of this dysfunction stems from chronic unethical behavior that starts in law school. From there, it only gets worse. A culture of greed, materialism, and unethical attitudes permeates many law firms. Again, Patrick Schiltz explains: "I tell my students that particularly if they go to work for a big law firm, they will probably begin to practice law unethically in at least some respects within their first year or two in practice."[69] He alleges that these are not just isolated instances but that the problem is built into the very fabric of modern-day law practice:

A young person who begins practicing law today will find herself immersed in a culture that is hostile to the values with which she was raised (unless she was raised to be rapaciously greedy), for the defining features of the legal profession today is obsession with money.... For the typical young attorney, acting unethically starts with her time sheets. One day, not too long after she starts practicing law, she will sit down at the end of a long day, and she just won't have much to show for her efforts in terms of billable hours. It will be near the end of the month. She will know that all of the partners will be looking at her monthly time reports in a few days, so what she'll do is pad her time sheet just a bit.

And then she will pad more and more…. And, before long, it won't take her much more than three or four years, she will be stealing from her clients almost every day…. The young lawyer's entire frame of reference will change. She will still be making dozens of quick instinctive decisions every day, but those decisions…will instead reflect…a set of values that embodies not what's right or wrong, but what is profitable, and what she can get away with.[70]

Add to that the soul-consuming notion of legal positivism. This philosophy encourages attorneys-turned-judges to expand their egos by basing decisions not on the restrictions of the Constitution and founding documents but upon their self-perceived "wisdom" and I-know-better-than-the-masses (i.e., you and me) elitist worldview.

U.S. Supreme Court Chief Justice Charles Evans Hughes said, "We are under a Constitution, but the Constitution is what the judges say it is."[71]

Whatever the judges may think it says or doesn't say, the Constitution says *nothing* about requiring that a member of the U.S. Supreme Court be an attorney. So I advocate it's time the judges' underclothing be changed.

We'd all be better off if the next few Supreme Court nominees have under their black robes the duds of a rancher, shirtsleeves of an entrepreneur, the uniform of a retired military officer, fireman, or policeman, the sweatsuit of a high school football coach, or whatever your favorite conservative talk-show host is wearing behind the microphone. Anything's better than a lawyer's thousand-dollar suit!

22

OVERTURNING THE OBJECTIVE
BASIS FOR LAW

Secular Humanism—and its core beliefs of moral relativism and Darwinian evolution—is the new, postmodern foundation on which America's courts and law schools are being built:

> Twentieth-century jurisprudence is based on a Darwinian world view. Life evolves, men evolve, society evolves, and therefore laws and the constitution's meaning evolves and changes with time.[72]

It's not meant to be this way, but there's a name for this new legal philosophy. It's called "legal positivism."

After reviewing the writings of the Critical Legal Studies movement—a group of radical lawyers, law professors, and law students—constitutional and legal scholar John Eidsmoe documents the implications of legal positivism:

> (1) There are no objective, God-given standards of law, or if there are, they are irrelevant to the modern legal system. (2) Since God is not the author of law, the author of law must be man; in other words, law is law simply because the highest human authority, the state, has said it is law and is able to back it up by force. (3) Since man and society evolve, therefore law must evolve as well. (4) Judges, through their decisions, guide the evolution of law (Note again: judges "make law"). (5) To study law, get at the original sources of law, the

decisions of judges; hence most law schools today use the "case law" method of teaching law.[73]

Legal positivism is essentially the application of the philosophy of moral relativism to the law. Moral relativism is the belief that there is no such thing as moral absolutes, no standard that is right or wrong for all people, in all places, at all times. Moral relativism is also known as pragmatism. It gives rise to situational ethics, the belief that individuals are free to decide for themselves what is best for them and what gives them the most desirable outcome in any given situation.

"This philosophy of 'positivism' was introduced in the 1870s when Harvard Law School Dean Christopher Columbus Langdell (1826-1906) applied Darwin's premise of evolution to jurisprudence."[74] It was further advanced by Dean Roscoe Pound and Supreme Court Justice Oliver Wendell Holmes, Jr. Holmes argued that there should be no fixed moral foundation for law:

> The felt necessities of the time, the prevalent moral and political theories...have a good deal more to do than the syllogism [legal reasoning process] in determining the rules by which men should be governed.[75]

That the "felt necessities of the time" and "prevalent moral and political theories" should be the basis of the rules by which men are governed is a shocking and dangerous premise. Such thinking has resulted in laws allowing countless abortions—including partial-birth abortions— in America. The late U.S. Senator Daniel Patrick Monahan called partial-birth abortion "near infanticide." Using "felt necessities of the time" and "prevalent moral and political theories" could allow most anything to be justifiable depending on whose feelings, morals, and political theories are in force.

To give you an example of how serious this situation has become: before becoming a U.S. Supreme Court justice, Ruth Bader Ginsburg, while serving on a lower court, wrote of her belief that the sex age limit should be lowered to twelve. If that is something enough judges "feel is a necessity," based the perverted "moral and political theories" of Alfred Kinsey, for instance, it could become legal.

This kind of preference could become law under postmodern thinking. Consider one other example of how it is already happening: the 2003 U.S. Supreme Court ruling, *Lawrence v. Texas*. In this case, the court struck down the sodomy law of Texas—and by implication those of several other states—making homosexual sex legal. The justices not only ignored the Constitution and the Founders' original intent, but they went so far as to cite the law of another country in making their case! I hope you'd have an objection to that.

23

THE PRIMARY PURPOSE OF
CIVIL GOVERNMENT

Kerby Anderson describes the significance of "Lex Rex,"
a renowned essay written by Samuel Rutherford on the
purpose of civil authority:

> Arguing that governmental law was founded on the law
> of God, he [Rutherford] rejected the seventeenth-cen-
> tury idea of the "divine right of kings." The king was
> not the ultimate authority, God's law was (hence the
> title Lex Rex, "The law is king"). If the king and the
> government disobeyed the law, then they were to be
> disobeyed. He argued that all men including the king
> were under God's law and not above it. According to
> Rutherford the civil magistrate was a "fiduciary figure"
> who held his authority in trust for the people. If that
> trust was violated, the people had a political basis for
> resistance. Not surprisingly "Lex Rex" was banned in
> England and Scotland because it was seen as treasonous
> and fomenting political rebellion.[76]

As I pointed out earlier, God set up the three distinct social
institutions of family, church, and state with differing realms of
responsibility and authority. Many Christians, though, mistakenly
believe that civil government always trumps church and family
authority. This false understanding has at times prompted Christians to offer more allegiance to civil government than to God by
reallocating the rightful responsibility and authority of family and

church governments to the state.

When civil government steps outside God's ordained purpose and persecutes righteous people, promotes evil, and fosters injustice on the innocent, the moral authority of civil government has been lost, and Christians are free to disobey. Disobedience to government may be required to oppose evil, promote righteousness, defend the weak, and provide for the safety of a person's family.

Kerby Anderson brilliantly describes the purpose of government as found in Romans 13:

> Some critics argue that civil disobedience is prohibited by the clear admonition in Romans 13:1, "Let every person be in subjection to the governing authorities. For there is not authority except from God, and those which exist are established by God" (NASB). Yet even this passage seems to provide a possible argument for disobeying a government that has exceeded its authority. The verses following these speak of the government's role and function. The ruler is to be a "servant of God," and government should reward good and punish evil. Government that fails to do so is outside God's mandated authority and function. Government is not autonomous; it has delegated authority from God. It is to restrain evil and punish wrongdoers. When it does violate God's delegated role and refuses to reward good and punish evil, it has not proper authority. The apostle Paul called for believers to "be subject" to government, but he did not instruct them to "obey" every command of government. When government issues an unjust or unbiblical injunction, Christians have a higher author-

ity. One can be "subject" to the authority of the state but still refuse to "obey" a specific law which is contrary to biblical standards.[77]

The late theologian Francis Schaeffer similarly warned, "One either confesses that God is the final authority, or one confesses that Caesar is Lord." We will serve God or serve man, but we cannot serve both. We obey government officials except when those authorities support civil laws that violate the laws of God.

First Peter 2:13-14 also makes it clear that God's plan for civil government is to punish evildoers and to protect and encourage those who do right: "Therefore submit yourselves to every ordinance of man for the Lord's sake, whether to the king as supreme, or to governors, as to those who are sent by him for the punishment of evildoers and for the praise of those who do good."

We live in a fallen world where people have a free will to do good or evil. While it is true that the church often flourishes during times of extreme persecution, this happens largely because of the civil disobedience of Christians who worship underground, smuggle Bibles, and distribute Scripture contrary to the laws governing them. Some governments are so evil, corrupt, and ungodly that Christians are obliged not to support them because to do so would be to participate in what they do.

According to Christ, the government should work in harmony with the church (Matthew 22:21), and when it does, God approves of the government in power. Understand, though, that church government is not necessarily superseded by civil government. Many people in the Bible took part in civil disobedience:

- When Pharaoh commanded the Hebrew midwives to kill all male Hebrew babies, Moses' mother lied to

Pharaoh and did not carry out his command (Exodus. 1-2);

- When Nebuchadnezzar ordered Shadrach, Meshach, and Abednego to bow down to his golden image, they refused and were cast into a fiery furnace (Daniel 3);

- Daniel prayed to God in spite of the king's dictate to the contrary (Daniel 6);

- In Acts, when Peter and John were commanded not to preach the gospel, their response was, "We ought to obey God rather than men" (Acts 5:29).[78]

We must do the same.

MONEY, MONEY EVERYWHERE

24

IT'S THE ECONOMY
(OF THE BIBLE), STUPID

When the Biblical principles on which the free enterprise system is based are put into practice, capitalism produces success for all who participate. But people who don't adopt Biblical principles of conduct and character won't reap the rewards of this system because it is based on personal responsibility.

When Biblical principles are ignored—or thwarted—the free enterprise system suffers and can even unravel. Just as socialism will not function in the long run because of mankind's sin nature, the free enterprise system can be hindered if people do not check their sinful tendencies. Unlike socialism, however, the free enterprise system offers such great rewards that people are encouraged to apply the principles that make the system effective.

Free enterprise works best when people are honest, moral, hard-working, responsible, conscientious, and selfless. Our system keeps on working because more people are honest than dishonest in most of their financial and business relationships. In addition to honesty, free enterprise is built on the Biblical principle of hard work. In 2 Thessalonians 3:6-12 Paul tells believers to follow his example of working so they don't have to rely on others to provide for them. He tells lazy folks to get to work or to starve.

Under socialism—where everyone is guaranteed an income—the government taxes citizens at exorbitant rates to support unmotivated people as well as the lavish lifestyles of the elite ruling class. As a result, there is little incentive to work, take risks, invest, save, to serve others, or to start a business.

The free enterprise system, on the other hand, rewards healthy self-interest. It is not only acceptable but Biblical to pursue what is in your best interest as long as you don't look after yourself at the expense or harm of someone else. These aspects of self-interest also have benefits to the others with whom you have relationships—your family, friends, co-workers, business acquaintances, and customers.

There are many things we do based on our best interest, and the free enterprise system rewards individuals who reject laziness in deference to working hard at a job, serving customers, and providing for their families. Honesty, hard work, a good reputation, and the promise of material blessings are the basis of the free enterprise system. It is not an accident that America became the wealthiest nation in the world. Biblical principles work—for Christians and non-Christians alike.

Unfortunately, free enterprise is naturally offensive to most humanists. Humanists don't want to be accountable to God and as a result always seek ways to thwart His laws. If humanists want to benefit financially without following God's laws, they're left with no choice but to turn to the state and relativism. Socialistic control is always the consequence.

While there are pitfalls in the free enterprise system, they are exaggerated when man's sinful nature or big government encroaches on or manipulates the free market. Kerby Anderson addresses some of the benefits of the free enterprise system as well as the arguments liberals make against it:

> Historically, capitalism has had a number of advantages. It has liberated economic potential. It has also

provided the foundation for a great deal of political and economic freedom. When government is not controlling markets, then there is economic freedom to be involved in a whole array of entrepreneurial activities.

Capitalism has led to a great deal of political freedom, because once you limit the role of government in economics, you limit the scope of government in other areas. It is no accident that most of the countries with the greatest political freedom usually have a great deal of economic freedom....

Capitalism is a system in which bad people can do the least harm, and good people have the freedom to do good works. Capitalism works well if you have completely moral individuals. But it also functions adequately when you have selfish and greedy people.[79]

The "magic" of capitalism is that serving others well ends up being in each person's best interest.

The Bible offers more than 2,000 verses on the subject of money. It discusses private property, private contracts, caring for the poor, laziness, staying out of debt, not being greedy, working for your food and investing for the future, leaving an inheritance to children, bribery, extortion, profit and loss, serving your customer, and much more. Here is a summary of the basic lessons from the Bible about money:

- Do not set your heart on riches, and especially be on your guard against oppression and robbery (Ps. 62:10; James 5:1-6).

- God calls us to be contented with what we have

rather than coveting what others have (Ex. 20:17; Heb. 13:5).

- If we place so much importance on money that we start loving it, we are liable to unleash all kinds of evil and sorrow (Ps. 52:1-7; Matt. 13:22; 1 Tim. 6:6-10; Rev. 3:17).

- Give God praise and thanks for any and all resources that you have, and honor Him by giving freely to others (Deut. 8:11, 17-18; Prov. 3:9-10; Matt. 10:8; Acts 20:35).

- Building your reputation around money is false; it can lead to dangerous and devastating results, as was the case for one couple in the early church (Acts 5:1-11).

- Wealth is a gift from God and should be received with thanksgiving, generosity, and stewardship (1 Tim. 6:17-18; 2 Cor. 8-9).[80]

In short, the most Biblical economic system is capitalism. Now that wasn't so hard was it?

25

FROM RICHES TO RAGS
THROUGH TAXATION

The *Humanist Manifestos* and the *Communist Manifesto* call for punishing wealthy people by requiring them to pay a higher tax rate. When the government takes from the rich through a punitive tax system, it is not only discourages work, but it is coveting—and acquiring—money to which it has no ethically legitimate claim.

Humanists generally want to redistribute wealth through some form of socialism, but their goal is not even possible. While money can be reallocated, the process never provides enough money to make everyone wealthy. When the government attempts to take from the rich to give to the "poor," they are taking capital from businesspeople who then are unable to expand their companies, start new companies, and create additional jobs to energize the economy. They are also less able to consume products themselves.

When fewer goods and services are purchased, people at all income levels suffer. If new cars remain on the sales lot, for instance, jobs are lost from the assembly line down to the car dealer. When home sales slump, wages disappear for the builder, the mortgage banker, realtor, home inspector, carpenter, concrete company, bricklayers, roofing company, landscapers, carpet layers, and movers. It is a fallacy to think the government can take by force from those with wealth in order to benefit the economy.

Consider another angle on the taxation issue as well. The Lord only asks for a 10% tithe of what we earn. Yet if God requests only 10% of our income for His work, why should the government need 50% or more? And, yes, the combination of federal and state income taxes, sales tax, tolls, airline, car, property, gasoline taxes, to name the most obvious, is far more than 50% for the average income earner in the United States. Even so, most Americans don't recognize how much they pay in taxes because many are "hidden taxes"—meaning people pay them without recognizing them as taxes (such as an amount figured into the purchase price of a product). Notice, too, that God did not set up a progressive tithing system where the more you make, the larger the percentage you tithe.

And despite federal ballyhooing about lower income taxes, the situation is getting worse. In 1960, the average taxpayer worked 36 days to pay all of his or her taxes, but by 2003, it took 189 days. That means American taxpayers now work more than half of each year just to pay their taxes![81]

Many Christians defend the government's unBiblical tax policies by citing Jesus' words that we should render unto Caesar what is Caesar's. The question arises, though, "What is Caesar's?" Is Caesar entitled to 50% of what you earn? That's certainly questionable. In addition, Jesus Christ was speaking of the Roman Empire. In America, *we* are Caesar in that ours is a government of the people, by the people, and for the people.

Not only is a progressive income tax unBiblical, so is the capital gains tax, as described by author, historian, and Worldview Weekend speaker, David Barton:

> The capital gains tax, which is a tax on profits, actually penalizes a person for success (i.e., the more profit a person makes, the higher the tax rate they pay) the more profit you make, the more you have to pay. How-

ever, in the Bible, the more profit you make, the more you are rewarded. Both the parable of the talents (Matthew 25:14-30) and the parable of the minas (Luke 19:12-27) conflict with the notion of a tax on capital gains. "For to everyone who has, more will be given, and he will have abundance; but from him who does not have, even what he has will be taken away." In other words, the Bible implies that those who do well (invest) with what they have will be given more.[82]

Further, it is a myth that the wealthy do not pay their share. A 2003 study reveals that 80% of taxes were paid by just 20% of Americans. In fact, here's how various income levels contribute to the tax collections in the United States:

- The top 5% pay 53% of all income taxes;
- the top 10% pay 65%;
- the top 25% pay 83%;
- the top 50% pay 96%;
- the bottom 50% pays a mere 4% of all income taxes.

In fact, the top 1% pays more than *ten times* the federal income tax as the bottom 50%! But note this:

- The top 1% earns only 17.5% of all income;
- the top 5% earns 32%;
- the top 10% earns 43%;
- the top 25% earns 65%;

- the top 50% earns 86% of the income.[83]

If you compare the breakdowns of taxes and incomes, you'll see that the higher income brackets pay far more than their share of taxes—in some cases, three times as much. If the tax structure were "flattened," they would still pay more tax than lower income people, but the burden would be fairly distributed. And the rich would have even more chance to share the wealth with all those "below" them who benefit from their investments.

26

SOCIALISM—
GUARANTEED POVERTY FOR ALL

The fundamental lie liberals believe—and propagate—about socialism and socialistic policies is that socialism will actually work if we just try it hard enough and long enough. This gives rise to all other lies about socialism, including the idea that it is a fair system by which to make sure everyone prospers.

The liberal love affair with socialism is deeply entrenched in the humanist mindset that denies anything like the all-too-evident tendency of people to do the wrong thing (the Christian worldview calls this "the sin nature of man"). In its Pollyanna fashion, socialism assumes the best about us, denying the reality that people routinely succumb to greed, selfishness, bitterness, dishonesty, and anger. That they are often awash in pride or envy. And that virtually anyone will be lazy if given the opportunity. All of these sinful human qualities undermine a system of economics based on equal work, equal income, and shared benefits. What "sin nature" requires is a system where overcoming these tendencies is in everyone's own best interests—namely, capitalism.

In his book *The Battle for Truth,* David Noebel explains the twisted thinking that makes people think socialism is viable:

> If one *denies* the inherent fallen nature of man, socialism becomes the most attractive economic system for creating a heaven on earth. For the Humanist, *there is*

no original sin to stand in the way of creating a helping, sharing, co-operative community on earth. Therefore, the economic system best suited to promote the ethics of Humanism and amend the evils of capitalism is socialism.[84] [emphasis mine]

There are even some non-liberals who mistakenly allow that the Bible endorses socialism. While many people described in the New Testament church shared their goods and livelihood, the key distinction is that theirs was a voluntary system, not a compulsory governmental system of sharing. Whenever government tries to equalize salaries or standards of living and education, productivity takes a nosedive.

The free enterprise system is the most equitable economic system available to our sin-prone humanity. Whereas socialism puts a few powerful elite in control of whether or not you have a job and how much money you make (for the benefit of the all-powerful state), capitalism offers to the individual control over his or her own earthly future, destiny, and wealth.

Few people realize that one of socialism's early failures took place right here in America's first colony. When the *Mayflower* set sail on August 1, 1620, it carried 102 passengers, including 40 Pilgrims led by William Bradford. During the first winter, half the Pilgrims (Bradford's wife among them) died of starvation, sickness, or exposure. When spring finally came, Indians taught the settlers to plant corn, fish for cod, and make beaver-skin coats. Life improved for the Pilgrims, but they did not yet prosper. Why?

The fault lay in the Pilgrims' original contract with their merchant-sponsors in London. The agreement required that everything the community produced go into a common store from which each member of the community was entitled to a share. All of the land they cleared and the houses they built also belonged to the group as a whole, not to individuals.

Bradford, who had become the governor of the colony, recognized that this form of collectivism was as destructive to the Pilgrims as their first harsh winter. In a bold break from the initial agreement, he assigned each family a plot of land that they would manage. Thus he unleashed the power of the marketplace. In his book *See I Told You So*, Rush Limbaugh summarizes the Pilgrim experience: "What Bradford and his community found was that the most creative and industrious people had no incentive to work any harder than anyone else, unless they could utilize the power of personal motivation!"[85]

Bradford himself also reckoned of their socialist experiment:

> …For this community [so far as it was] found to breed much confusion and discontent, and retard much employment that would have been to their benefit and comfort. For young men that were most able and fit for labor and service did repine that they should spend their time and strength to work for other men's wives and children without any recompense…that was thought injustice.[86]

So, long before Karl Marx was even born, the Pilgrims experimented with socialism and quickly discovered its ruinous consequences.

America was fortunate to have early pioneers brave not only the wilds but also misguided social experiments. If we remember the lessons, we may save ourselves from disaster. Lacking such benefit, the former Soviet Union may never recover from the years of socialism that kept it from becoming prosperous and advanced. Of course, liberals—patriots that they claim to be—may yet convince enough of us to follow in Marxist rather than Pilgrim footsteps. Or should we say *missteps*?

27

STATE-SPONSORED GAMBLING—
GOOD FUN AND FINANCIAL OBLIVION FOR ALL

We could give liberals the benefit of the doubt and think that when they say lotteries are "good for the economy" they're using the phrase in a relative sense. It's good, for instance, if you're a state politician touting a rise in gambling revenues, but it's bad if you're the state accounting office paying out more unemployment and other welfare-related claims. Or it's good if you're a college student adding lottery money to your tuition account, but it's bad if you're the indigent family whose minimum-wage income earners are weekly forking over their kids' milk money to buy lottery tickets. Or again, it's good if you're the convenience store owner making your share on ticket sales, but it's bad if you're the family crushed by a $30,000 debt brought on by the compulsive gambler who is the convenience store's best customer.

So "good" actually is a very relative term, and in this case, it's relatively bad.

Apparently, historian John Ezel agrees. In his book *Fortune's Merry Wheel* he concludes, "If history teaches us anything, a study of over 1,300 legal lotteries held in the United States proves…they cost more than they brought in if their total impact on society is reckoned."[87]

When you start reviewing the items on the "total impact on society" list, it's fairly stunning. One pastor I know came up with this array of astounding statistics in his attempt to convince his congregation to oppose state-sponsored gambling:

- In one year, more than $550 billion is spent in legalized gambling. Each day, $88 million is spent on lotteries alone—more than is spent on food.

- Ten million Americans have a gambling addiction. When gamblers come to the point of seeking help, their debts range between $18,000 and $50,000.

- When legalized gambling enters a new area, there is a 100- to 500-percent rise in the instance of compulsive gamblers. At least two-thirds of compulsive gamblers turn to crime to finance their addiction.

- One county in Mississippi had an increase of 500 divorces after a gambling casino opened there.

- A Colorado city realized a six-fold increase in child protection cases the year after a casino arrived.

- 20 percent of compulsive gamblers attempt suicide.

Even *U.S. News & World Report* joined the bandwagon: "Crime rates are higher in places with gambling: 1,092 incidents per 10,000 population in 1994, compared with 593 per 10,000 for the entire nation." And by the way, higher crime rates *aren't* good for the economy, and they *do* hurt people.

Despite the devastating impact of gambling on Americans, many lawmakers continue to support legislation that allows for the proliferation of gambling. Thankfully, some do oppose gambling legislation because they understand the real economic liability and dangerous social impact.

In addition to the obvious bitter consequences of gambling,

there are two fundamental reasons stemming from a Biblical worldview as to why gambling is wrong.

(1) The lottery uses deception and as a result is essentially a form of legalized robbery.

Every TV or radio commercial promoting a state lottery or a casino purports to offer you a genuine opportunity to become wealthy. But you have a better chance of being struck by lightning than of getting rich playing the lottery. And how many women do you know who have borne quadruplets? If you have 705,000 female acquaintances who are mothers, one may well be a mother of quadruplets. Yet having quadruplets is a sure bet compared to your chances of winning the "big one" in the lottery (1 in 12,912,583).[88]

How many lottery commercials present the sad and devastating consequences that gambling has on marriages and children? Whoops. Guess they forgot to mention that. No, lottery ads only promise you a great time, lots of fun and happiness, and, of course, piles of cash.

(2) Gambling takes advantage of the poor.

Numerous studies show beyond a doubt that those who pay the dearest price for the vice of gambling are people in low-income families:

> Lotteries "are more aggressive than most other forms of gambling, since individuals in lower income brackets spend proportionally more money on them than do persons with higher income," according to the National Policy on Gambling.

> In Georgia, those who make less than $25,000 a

year spend three times as much on lottery tickets as those who make $75,000 or more per year. On the national average, lottery gamblers with household incomes under $10,000 bet nearly three times as much on the lottery as those with incomes of more than $50,000.[89]

Casinos, lottery tickets, pull-tabs at the local bar, online gambling, and horse tracks seem to have become the great American pastime. And many misguided folks whistle happy tunes about the great benefits we all reap from those who chase the pipe dream of getting rich through gambling. Unfortunately, the benefit of the doubt I offered at the beginning of this chapter ends up being of no benefit to society.

28

THE POOR AMONG US
INSTALLMENT 1

Ruling classes throughout history have found ways to oppress the less fortunate. Americans, though, pride themselves on being above all that now—feudal lords, serfdom, slavery, or even the more sophisticated modern versions like Communist ruling party domination of everyone else. But the "intellectual elite" of America have found a far more insidious means than mere brute force to oppress the down and out, to assure the continued misery of millions. A decades-long brainwashing by liberal-leaning social engineers has so altered the worldview of the underclass that they have little choice but to live in the mire of their culturally bankrupt caste.

Psychiatrist Theodore Dalrymple, author of the book *Life at the Bottom: The Worldview that Makes the Underclass*, has spent years treating the poor in a slum hospital and prison in England. So just why is the condition of the underclass so oppressive? While Dr. Dalrymple's is not a Christian book per se, he nevertheless arrives at the astounding conclusion that a misshapen worldview accounts for the plight of today's poor in Western countries:

> Patterns of behavior emerge—in the case of the underclass, almost entirely self-destructive ones. Day after day I hear of the same violence, the same neglect and abuse of children, the same broken relationships, the same victimization by crime, the same nihilism, the

same dumb despair. If everyone is a unique individual, how do patterns such as this emerge?

Dalrymple later answers his own question:

> Welfare states have existed for substantial periods of time without the development of a modern underclass: an added ingredient is obviously necessary. This ingredient is to be found in the realm of ideas. Human behavior cannot be explained without reference to the meaning and intentions people give their acts and omissions; and everyone has a *Weltanschauung*, a worldview, whether he knows it or not. It is the ideas my patients have that fascinate—and, to be honest, appall—me: for they are the source of their misery.[90]

While there are a few true *victims* of poverty—children who suffer from their parents' bad choices (which all too many choose to repeat as adults)—the blame for poverty does not lie solely with those who make lifestyle decisions that lead to their status. Dr. Dalrymple asserts that the great facilitators of chronic indigence are liberal humanists and their worldview of "if it feels good do it": "most of the social pathology exhibited by the underclass has its origin in ideas that have filtered down from the intelligentsia."[91]

"Intelligentsia" is a synonym for liberal, humanistic elite—educrats and social engineers. Propagation of the liberal, morally relativistic worldview has raged through the underclass most ruinously in the form of glaring sexual promiscuity. Remember what the humanist manifestos have to say about moral relativism, sex, and the pursuit of pleasure:

• *Humanist Manifesto I*: "...the quest for the good life is still the central task for mankind."

• *Humanist Manifesto II*: "We strive for the good life, here and now.... neither do we wish to prohibit, by law or social sanction, sexual behavior between consenting adults. The many varieties of sexual exploration should not in themselves be considered 'evil.'"

Dalrymple articulates the agonizing consequences reaped by the underclass because they embraced, however unwittingly, the worldview of humanists:

> Of nothing is this more true than the system of sexual relations that now prevails in the underclass, with the result that 70 percent of the births in my hospital are now illegitimate (a figure that would approach 100 percent if it were not for the presence in the area of a large number of immigrants from the Indian subcontinent).
>
> ...The connection between this loosening and the misery of my patients is so obvious that it requires considerable intellectual sophistication (and dishonesty) to be able to deny it.
>
> The climate of moral, cultural, and intellectual relativism—a relativism that began as a mere fashionable plaything for intellectuals—has been successfully communicated to those least able to resist its devastating practical effects.[92]

Do ideas have consequences? Does your worldview matter? Liberals can enjoy the distinct satisfaction of seeing just how radically their "forward-thinking" ideas affect the world in which people live day by day. Isn't the compassion of unrestrained sexual expression, of ongoing handouts to the needy, a wonderful thing?

Anyone who regards with even a shred of honesty the destruction of unregenerate people in the underclass knows the liberals' time is up. Their social experiment is as bust as the former Soviet Union's Communism. The Christian worldview is the hope that is left—and a genuine hope it is. Christians must reach out to the underclass, seek to change hearts, renew minds, and reframe their deformed worldview by showing them the need for Christ. But that is a discussion worthy of a chapter in itself—my next one.

29

THE POOR AMONG US
INSTALLMENT 2

To be sure, Jesus promised that the poor will "always be with us." A key reason is man's sinful nature, and one all-too-common consequence of sin is poverty.

It is crucial to understand that sometimes when the Bible speaks of the poor, Scripture is referring to a person's spiritual, not financial, condition. However, when the Bible does discuss the fiscally poor, it is not the American definition of the term. Biblical poverty refers to someone who does not have a coat, food or shelter. Often in America those the government says live in poverty not only have a home, an apartment, and a coat but a color television, cable TV, video games, an automobile, beer, cigarettes, lottery tickets, and other comforts as well.

In the previous chapter I cited Theodore Dalrymple's well-reasoned view that liberal, humanistic philosophies have guaranteed us a chronic underclass. The worldview foisted upon the down-and-out by elites has fostered an epidemic of bad choices among those living in poverty. As a result, a large number of the indigent reap misery from what they have sowed. Nevertheless, Christians must reach out to them, offering a worldview that calls them to personal responsibility and adherence to a godly moral code.

I know from firsthand experience that Dr. Dalrymple's observations are true. For five years on the first Tuesday of each month, I traveled to the Union Gospel Mission in St. Paul, Minnesota, to speak and lead music for the nightly service before the mission's free supper. Except for the few mentally ill regulars left on the streets after the death of a parent who had cared for them, I met individuals that choose to be homeless. In fact, most have a home and parents, or even a wife and children, but they opt to live awash in drugs, alcohol, serial sexual encounters—in short, a life of no responsibility. Many men who showed up for the service (attendance required if they wanted the free meal) admitted that they choose to live as they do.

The mission chaplain told me numerous personal stories of habitual attendees who could return to their families if they would simply take responsibility for their actions, clean themselves up, get a job, and stop abusing drugs and alcohol. There were men, he explained, who at one time had been judges, doctors, attorneys, or businessmen who destroyed their lives through drugs and booze.

Regardless of how the patrons get there, though, countless Union Gospel Missions across the nation do the work of the Lord in ministering to and assisting those who want help getting off drugs or alcohol and landing a job. Yes, there are those who abuse the missions, but once we step into the trenches of the war on poverty, the legitimate victories are worth the occasions of being "had." I believe firmly that Christians should financially support and volunteer at local missions to the homeless.

Even individuals who have made poor decisions and are reaping the consequences sometimes surprise us—thanks be only to God!—by changing. I have seen more than one such person come to Christ, and I have watched as a life is transformed in the way only having a personal relationship with Jesus can do. These people need our support and encouragement—God's mercy and grace expressed through us—as they strive to put their lives together and become productive citizens.

They rightfully need our friendship and financial support. A word of caution, though: Don't just hand them cash. Take them shopping and purchase for them the things they need. This not only shows you care, but—unlike handing them dollars that can be mismanaged—it gives them much-needed accountability. If you can't take them shopping, give them a gift card to a department store, and tell them you want to know what they buy. Explain that they should purchase things to build a personal "infrastructure," the everyday items essential to bettering their lot—a coat or dress, pants, cookware—and let them know you will be excited to see what they come up with. This teaches in a small step how to wisely manage life.

Outside of missions, there is also a great realm of people genuinely needing help. My personal favorite is older adults raising grandchildren because parents have abandoned the kids. These sweet grandmothers and grandfathers are the modest daily heroes among us.

Many of the poor have made bad choices and suffer the consequences, but we all have made personally destructive decisions in one way or another. I'm grateful for God's grace, mercy, forgiveness, and compassion, and I believe I honor the Lord by treating others as He has treated me. Some people truly don't deserve our help or compassion, but then, God loved each of us before we loved Him. As we muse over how to handle the poor among us, we do well to remember Martin Luther's famous call to humility in our judgments: There but for the grace of God go I.

MODERN THINKING—
DON'T BUY IT

30

THE "NEUTRAL" RELIGION
OF SECULARISTS

Let's get straight to the point on this one. Secularists have been cramming humanism down the throats of America's school children for at least two generations, the result of a long-term strategy to substitute Secular Humanism for traditional religion. In 1930, Charles Francis Potter spelled out the tactic in his book, *Humanism: A New Religion:*

> Education is thus a most powerful ally of Humanism, and every American public school is a school of Humanism. What can the theistic Sunday schools, meeting for an hour once a week, and teaching only a fraction of the children do to stem the tide of a five-day program of humanistic teaching?[93]

John J. Dunphy, an aggressive humanist, echoed a similar approach in an essay for *The Humanist:*

> I am convinced that the battle for human kind's future must be waged and won in the public school classroom by teachers.... These teachers must embody the same selfless dedication of the most rabid fundamentalist preachers. For they will be ministers of another sort, utilizing a classroom instead of a pulpit to convey humanist values in whatever subject they teach, regardless of the education level—preschool, day care, or large state university. The classroom must and will become an arena of conflict between the old and the

new; the rotting corpse of Christianity, together with all its adjacent evils and misery, and the new faith of humanism. Humanism will emerge triumphant. It must if the family of humankind is to survive.[94]

Brooks Alexander saw this clearly when he observed:

> In the ideological contest for cultural supremacy, public education is the prime target; it influences the most people in the most pervasive way at the most impressionable age. No other social institution has anything close to the same potential for mass indoctrination.[95]

Our alleging of this specific and strategic targeting of America's educational system by liberal humanists is not based on isolated cases, either. The concept is accepted even at a popular level as evidenced by Marilyn Ferguson's *The Aquarian Conspiracy*. Ferguson surveyed New Agers (also known as Cosmic Humanists), and her study reveals, "more were involved in education than in any other single category of work. They were teachers, administrators, policy makers, and educational psychologists." Feminist *and* humanist, Gloria Steinem adds her assessment: "... we will, I hope, raise our children to believe in human potential, not God."

One-time Nebraska State Senator Peter Hoagland, who later was elected to the U.S. Congress, debated a Nebraska pastor and administrator of a Christian school. Peter Hoagland bemoaned the influence that a Christian school education has on children:

> What we are most interested in, of course, are the children themselves. I don't think any of us in the legis-

lature have any quarrel with the right of the reverend or the members of his flock to practice their religion, but we don't think that they should be entitled to impose decisions or religious philosophies on their children which could seriously undermine those children's ability to deal in this complicated world when they grow up.[96]

So has this school indoctrination campaign been successful? In a word: Yes. In several words: Frighteningly so, and it has been working well for quite some time.

Consider that in 1986, Paul C. Vitz conducted a study of America's schools and textbooks. Funded by the federal government's National Institute of Education (under the Department of Education), Vitz documented that the Secular Humanist worldview dominates the nation's textbooks and that the Christian worldview is excluded: "[A] very widespread secular and liberal mindset...pervades the leadership of education (and textbook publishing) and a secular and liberal bias is its inevitable consequence."[97]

He even notes that the Christian worldview has been specifically censored:

> High school books covering U.S. history were also studied, and none came close to adequately presenting the major religious events of the past 100 to 200 years. Most disturbing was the constant omission of reference to the large role that religion has always played in American life. This fact has been seen as a fundamental feature of American history by foreign observers since de Tocqueville.[98]

Vitz also analyzed 670 stories and articles from grades 3 to 6. A small number had religion as a secondary theme, but no story featured Christian or Jewish religious motivations. There was not a single reference to Protestant religious life. Religion was the main theme of one story, however: American Indian religion was central in the life of an American white girl. A social studies book offered some 30 pages on the Pilgrims, including a discussion of the first Thanksgiving, but there was not one word or image that referred to religion as being any part of the Pilgrims' life. One mother whose son's class was using this book wrote to me saying her son came home and explained that "Thanksgiving was when the Pilgrims gave thanks to the Indians."

Vitz draws an ominous conclusion regarding the influence of humanism on America's educational system:

> Given the overwhelming secular philosophies characterizing American education in the last fifty years, it is to be expected that leaders in education will differ markedly from the general American public in the area of basic moral values....
>
> Whether one calls it secular humanism, enlightenment universalism, skeptical modernism, or just plain permissive liberalism, the bottom line is that a very particular and narrow sectarian philosophy has taken control of American education.[99]

But at least they're neutral.

31

HUMANISM AS RELIGION—
IT QUALIFIES

Webster's New World Dictionary defines religion as "a system of belief,"[100] and "belief" is defined as "opinions and thoughts upon which people base their actions."[101] Since a person's worldview is the foundation of his or her values, and these values form the basis for a person's actions, humanism qualifies as a religious worldview. It supplies the belief system on which humanists base their actions.

Unfortunately, most Americans don't realize humanism is a religion that is promoted in America's public schools with taxpayer funds. While the ACLU and their ilk fight to remove the religion of Christianity from our schools, colleges, courtrooms, city halls, city seals, or the city square, their dirty little secret is that they really don't want a religion-free zone. They want to replace the Judeo-Christian faith and acknowledgment of God's place in our history with their religion of Secular Humanism.

Humanism had its beginning in the Garden of Eden when Satan deceived Adam and Eve into believing that if they would eat from the Tree of the Knowledge of Good and Evil they would be like God. Early on, mankind bought into the lie of humanism.

Dr. David Noebel and Dr. Tim LaHaye, in their 2003 *New York Times* best-seller *Mind Siege*, wrote:

> The truth is, humanism is unmistakably and demonstrably a religion. One need merely visit the second edition of *A World Religions Reader* to note the prominence

given to Secular Humanism as one of the world's religions. Indeed, in a list of the world's religions—Hinduism, Buddhism, Shintoism, Judaism, Christianity, Islam, and Sikhism—secular humanism is at the top.[102]

Some argue that humanism—unlike Christianity—does not force a specific set of religious positions and beliefs on people. But Dr. Noebel counters:

> Humanists preach a faith every bit as dogmatic as Christianity. Moral relativism is foundational for Secular Humanist ethics; spontaneous generation and evolution are basic to their biology; naturalism is foundational to their philosophy; and atheism is their theological perspective.[103]

In 1961, the Supreme Court handed down the *Torcaso v. Watkins* decision regarding a Maryland notary public who was initially disqualified from office because he would not declare a belief in God. The Court, however, ruled in his favor. It argued that "theistic religions [religions that believe in one God] could not be favored by the Court over non-theistic religions. In a footnote it clarified what it meant by non-theistic religions."[104] In the footnote, Justice Hugo L. Black wrote, "Among religions in this country which do not teach what would generally be considered a belief in the existence of God are Buddhism, Taoism, Ethical Culture, Secular Humanism, and others."[105]

Slam dunk! The Court's footnote acknowledging humanism as a religion laid the groundwork for multiple lawsuits that have allowed conservatives to stop the federal funding of humanism in our schools, right?

Wrong.

Dr. Noebel, a regular keynote speaker at the Worldview Weekends, bemoans the Court's double standard. Decisions often give the religion of humanism a free pass while stripping away the religious freedoms of more and more Christians under a misinterpretation of the First Amendment. He notes:

> Unfortunately, the Court has not been consistent in applying this understanding to its present interpretation of the First Amendment. If the no-establishment clause of the First Amendment really means that there should be a "wall of separation" between church and state, why are only theistic religions disestablished? If Secular Humanism is a religion—something the U.S. Supreme Court has claimed, and something countless Humanists proclaim—why is it allowed access to our public schools when there is to be no established religion?[106]

The dirty little secret of humanists is that they know humanism is a religion, but they will deny it when it puts at risk the federal tax dollars Congress appropriates to fund humanist-leaning textbooks and programs in America. Not only that, but many members of Congress know exactly what is going on. Most American citizens, though, are simply unaware and continue through the allocation of their tax dollars to establish a religion—the religion of humanism. Even the Internal Revenue Service has recognized it as a religion for years. Numerous humanist organizations, including the American Humanist Association, have a "religious" tax exemption.

Many churches and Christians have merged a humanist worldview with Christianity. Scripture also foretells this apostasy within the church. The falling away from traditionally held Biblical truths will lay the foundation for an apostate church to accept false teachings in the last days, about which the Bible has much to say.

Finally, the *Humanist Manifesto I* acknowledges that everything is a religious issue: "The distinction between the sacred and the secular can no longer be maintained."

I rest my case. Humanists know they're religious about their beliefs.

32

WILL THE REAL FAMILY VALUES
PLEASE STAND UP?

Of course liberal politicans support traditional family values—as long as you define family as anything from a husband, wife, and ten kids to two homosexual men living together. And, yes, they believe in parental authority—if it doesn't interfere with pluralistic indoctrination in public schools and the oversight of social workers. Society, they may allow, is glad for people to have kids (2.1 of them, anyway), but once they're in daylight, it's time for the government to raise them as it sees fit.

And what is "fitting" by government standards? In various education policy manuals and literature, I have seen children described as "human resource" and the parents described as "the supplier of the raw material."[107] Doesn't that give you the warm fuzzies!

How many parents who may otherwise buy into public education have considered what it means to be the "supplier"? As in any manufacturing process, once you provide the raw material, it's up to the production experts to make something meaningful out of the resource.

Former Arizona Superintendent of Public Instruction Carolyn Warner certainly does not hide her opinion when it comes to the value and importance of parents:

> Those who educate are more to be honored than those
> who bear the children. The latter gave them only life,

the former teach them the art of living.[108]

Feminist leader Gloria Steinem once proudly outlined the goal of radical humanists such as herself. In an interview with *Saturday Education* in 1973, she explained:

> The point is to enlarge personal choice, to produce for each child the fullest possible range of human experience without negating or limiting the choices already made by the adults' closest to her or him.[109]

So who are these close adults beyond whose choices we are expanding the children's? Mom and Dad, of course. According to Steinem, it is crucial that we let children know their beliefs and values do not have to line up with those of their parents.

This isn't just about giving kids a choice. No, liberals want to change the minds of children, to prevent them from growing up to be conservative—or even worse—God-fearing adults. The child's "right to choose" should be enforced by laws and policies to make sure children are not taught a worldview with which the intellectual elite don't agree.

Syndicated columnist Thomas Sowell notes how educators and social engineers view parents:

> Central to this questioning of authority is a questioning of the role of the central authority in the child's life—parents. Alternative ways of constructing individual values, independently of parental values, are recurring themes of curriculum materials on the most disparate subjects, from sex to death.[110]

Children are taught that their values should not be derived from a parent's Christian worldview but from their own feelings and desires, spiced generously with those of peers and teachers.

But why this radical humanist preoccupation with under-mining parental authority? Because otherwise (naturally) the in-fluence of parents is overwhelming, and very few American fathers and mothers actually embrace a humanist worldview. Therefore, parents need to be moved out of the picture. Once again, Sowell makes the issue very clear:

> Parents are the greatest obstacle to any brainwashing of children, and it is precisely the parents' values which are to be displaced. If parents cannot be gotten out of the picture or at least moved to the periphery, the whole brainwashing operation is jeopardized. Not only will individual parents counter what the brainwashers say; parents as a group can bring pressure to bear against the various psychological conditioning programs, and in some places get them forced out of the schools.[111]

With that in mind, perhaps it is understandable why liber-als want so much to make their version of society to stick. After all, "family values" are much easier to sell than a psychological conditioning program.

33

PLANNED PARENTHOOD
OR PLANNED RACISM?

*At the time this book was published, 44 million
American babies had been murdered through the
1973 U.S. Supreme Court ruling Roe v. Wade
that legalized abortion.*

I have studied the lives of many people, but Margaret Sanger is one of the most vile, evil, mean, and racist of all. Liberal professors and media outlets that have anything positive to say about Planned Parenthood or Margaret Sanger prove themselves to be extremely ignorant, racist, or both.

After divorcing her first husband and the father of her three children, Margaret Sanger became the publisher of a liberal newspaper she called *The Woman Rebel*. The slogan for her paper was "No Gods! No Masters!" Indeed, as a member of the Socialist Party, she was a rebel in more ways than one could count.[112]

The first issue of Sanger's paper denounced marriage as a "degenerate institution," capitalism as "indecent exploitation," and sexual modesty as "obscene prudery." In the next issue, an article entitled "A Woman's Duty" stated that "rebel women" were to "look the whole world in the face with a go-to-hell look in their eyes."[113]

In issues to follow, she published articles on sexual liberation, social revolution, contraception, and two articles that defended political assassinations. Sanger was served with a subpoena indicting her on three counts for publication of lewd and indecent articles. She fled to England, where she became acquainted with the eugenics movement, and she spent a year there before returning to the U.S. (Eugenicists, as defined by Dr. George Grant are "the practitioners of an odd pseudo-science who sincerely believe that if human civilization were to survive, the physically unfit, the materially poor, the spiritually diseased, the racially inferior, and the mentally incompetent had to be eliminated."[114])

Once back home, Sanger organized a public relations campaign to have all charges against her dropped. She began to put her eugenic worldview into practice by opening a birth control clinic in Brownsville, New York. This area was inhabited by Slavic, Latino, Italian, and Jewish immigrants. Sanger stated that these ethnic groups were "dysgenic and diseased races" that needed to have their "reckless breeding" curbed.[115] Barely two weeks after the clinic opened, it was shut down. Sanger and her sister were sentenced to 30 days in a workhouse for distributing obscene material and prescribing dangerous medical procedures.

Shortly after her release, she started an organization called the Birth Control League which published a magazine entitled *Birth Control Review*. A huge success, the publication not only garnered many paying subscriptions that generated revenue to further Sanger's cause, but it also attracted the attention and donations of famous and wealthy donors.

Sanger became acquainted with the doctors and scientists that had worked with Nazi Germany's "race purification" program and had no quarrel with the euthanasia, sterilization, abortion, and infanticide programs of the early Reich.[116] Sanger even published several articles in *Birth Control Review* that reflected Hilter's White Supremacist worldview.[117]

Within a few years, Sanger had authored several best-selling books and was speaking to large and receptive audiences, not only in America but all over the world. She was a celebrity with a following. In her book *The Pivot of Civilization*, Sanger praised the cause of eugenics, openly calling for the eradication of "human weeds,"[118] for the "cessation of charity,"[119] for the segregation of "morons, misfits, and the maladjusted,"[120] and for the coercive sterilization of "genetically inferior races."[121]

Sanger married a multimillionaire who eagerly funded her cause. Not wanting to find herself in trouble with the law, she opened a new clinic but called it a "Research Bureau." She received large grants from foundations such as Rockefeller, Ford, and Mellon.[122]

After World War II, the horrors of Hitler and his Nazi doctors and scientists came to light, and Sanger had to work fast to remake her image and distance herself from them. To accomplish this goal, she started a new organization with a new name: Planned Parenthood. Sanger was successful in hiding her racism and bigotry behind family-friendly names such as Planned Parenthood and family planning. Family planning means today what it meant in Sanger's day—abortion on demand. But make no mistake, for those who want to do the research, the evidence is there that Margaret Sanger was a racist and a bigot.

With all this historical evidence, it is remarkable that the Democratic Party continues to align itself with Planned Parenthood while it still manages to attract the majority of non-white voters. The fact that the liberal media and liberal educators don't join me in exposing Planned Parenthood's racist's worldview, but instead promotes and partners with them speaks volumes.

If you think Planned Parenthood has rejected its racist roots, then you're mistaken. Dr. Alan Guttmacher, the man who directly followed Sanger as the president of Planned Parenthood, said, "We are merely walking down the path that Mrs. Sanger carved out for us." Fate Wattleton was president of the organization during the 1980s, and she said she was "proud" to be "walking in the footsteps" of Sanger. In 1994, the president of Planned Parenthood was Pamela Maraldo who said, "Today, Planned Parenthood proudly carries on the courageous tradition of Margaret Sanger." [123]

So if you're ever sitting in class and the professor or your liberal classmates start singing the praises of Margaret Sanger or Planned Parenthood, ask them when they became supporters of racism, bigotry, anti-Semitism, and Nazism. Also ask why they're opposed to women's rights. After all, abortion in America has denied millions of little women the right to life.

34

JUDGMENT CALLS, OK?

Tolerance mongers seem to have found the one absolute truth they are willing to live by: "Judge not, lest you be judged." It sounds delightfully convenient for their cause. The statement has become the great American open-mindedness mantra when anyone has the courage to declare that someone else's beliefs, actions, or lifestyle are morally amiss.

Another form of the same non-judgmental judgment is "that may be true for you, but it's not true for me." The logic behind the statement goes something like this: "Your truth is your truth, and my truth is my truth. We are both right, and I hold to my opinion of truth." The last time I checked, though, it was impossible for two chairs to occupy the same space around my dining room table, but evidently such rules of time, space, and logic don't apply to tolerance philosophy.

Postmodernism's live-and-let-live concept of truth argues that even two opposite and wholly contradictory claims can both be true. This is as stupid as saying that black and white are the same color. Yet, it clarifies the absurdity of the postmodernism we are all supposed to blithely accept as the fundamental principle by which we respond to each other's ideas.

So beware. If you dare claim that another person's "truth"—whether it be about abortion, war, euthanasia, or capital punishment—is not, in fact, truth but is, in fact, *wrong*, you are not only being intolerant, but you are also being (mantra forbid!) judgmental.

In his book, *True for You, But Not for Me*, Paul Copan describes the fallacy in this all too common thinking:

> It has been said that the most frequently quoted Bible verse is no longer John 3:16 but Matthew 7:1: "Do not judge, or you too will be judged." We cannot glibly quote this, though, without understanding what Jesus meant. When Jesus condemned judging, he wasn't at all implying we should never make judgments about anyone. After all, a few verses later, Jesus himself calls certain people "pigs" and "dogs" (Matt 7:6) and "wolves in sheep's clothing" (7:15). ... What Jesus condemns is a critical and judgmental spirit, an unholy sense of superiority. Jesus commanded us to examine ourselves first for the problems we so easily see in others. Only then can we help remove the speck in another's eye— which, incidentally, assumes that a problem exists and must be confronted.[124]

Those who tell you not to judge, quoting Matthew 7:1 grossly out of context, are often the most mean-spirited, judgmental souls you could ever meet. It is not, of course, that they don't want anyone to judge anything, because they want very much to judge and condemn your commitment to lovingly speak and practice your Christian worldview. You see how these tolerance rules work? We must tolerate them, but they don't have to tolerate us. The logic is consistent, anyway.

Today's postmodern culture of adults and students is so consumed with non-judgmentalism that there are some who say we should not even call wrong or evil the terrorists that attacked America on September 11, 2001. In a *Time* magazine essay entitled "God Is Not on My Side. Or Yours," Roger Rosenblatt offers the philosophical underpinnings of the accommodation rule for global terrorism:

> One would like to think that God is on our side against the terrorists, because the terrorists are wrong and we are in the right, and any deity worth his salt would be able to discern that objective truth. But this is simply good-hearted arrogance cloaked in morality—the same kind of thinking that makes people decide that God created humans in his own image. The God worth worshipping is the one who pays us the compliment of self-regulation, and we might return it by minding our own business.[125]

If Americans don't start to judge and punish evil instead of accepting all ideas and beliefs as equal, we will become a nation that welcomes same-sex marriage, polygamy, pedophilia, incest, euthanasia, and likely a host of moral aberrations so bizarre they're still hidden in the darkest reaches of the Internet. We head a little further that way every time you hear someone say, "You know we are not to judge people; even the Bible says, 'judge not, lest you be judged'."

35

POSTMODERNISM—THE WORLDVIEW THAT WILL DESTROY AMERICA

Liberals assault absolute truth by proclaiming that all truth is relative. Every man and woman must decide what is right or wrong based on each situation he or she encounters.

Postmodernism is the belief that truth and reality are not discovered by man but are created by man. People create truth when they survey a situation and choose a course of action that will give the best results. This idea comes from the humanist worldview that proclaims mankind as the measure of all things. Therefore, each person is free to do what is in his or her own best interest.

This is exactly why you will hear someone say, "That may be true for you, but it is not true for me." A postmodern worldview actually allows two opposing truth claims to be equal—unless the opposing worldview is based on a fixed, moral standard. Such an opposing view is not seen by the postmodernist as being equal but as actually being unacceptable and intolerant.

The Christian believes that God created truth for man to discover and that God's truth is for all times, all places, and all people. The Biblical view also holds that men and women will be held accountable by God at the end of life for what they did with that truth.

To the postmodern humanist, Christianity is the devil, the cause of all the problems in our society and the world. The Christian worldview slows progress, prohibits equality, and sabotages world peace. In a postmodern, humanist worldview there is no tolerance for Christianity. In fact, it is not only acceptable for humanists to be intolerant of Christians and Christianity, it is their duty.

Postmodernists claim that each culture or community is free to determine what is right or wrong. Stanley J. Grenz points out in his book *A Primer on Postmodernism* that "truth is relative to the community in which a person participates. And since there are many communities, there are necessarily many different truths."[126]

This postmodern thinking is now accepted by far too many people. In a *U.S. News & World Report* article, Professor Robert Simon acknowledges that he's never met a student who denies the reality of the Holocaust, but what he hears is almost as disturbing:

> What he sees quite often, though, is worse: students who acknowledge the fact of the Holocaust but who can't bring themselves to say that killing millions of people is wrong.... "Of course, I dislike the Nazis," one student told Simon, "but who is to say they are morally wrong?" Overdosing on non-judgmentalism is a growing problem in the schools. Two disturbing articles in the *Chronicle of Higher Education* say that some students are unwilling to oppose large moral horrors, including human sacrifice, ethnic cleansing and slavery, because they think that no one has the right to criticize the moral views of another group or culture.

Now why would students say they don't agree with Hitler but can't say what he did was wrong? America's educational system has been so successfully infiltrated with moral relativism, situational ethics, and a postmodern worldview that students cannot bring themselves to say that what Hitler did was *wrong*.

Ultimately, this line of thinking runs aground on the very nature of truth itself. Truth is not "what" but "who." God Himself is truth. Jesus made this clear in John 14:6—"I am the way, the truth, and the life." And that's a reality we can all live with.

36

FREE TO BE RIGHT, WRONG, OR WHATEVER

In 1992, an earthquake occurred in American political philosophy that registered about a 9.7 on the Richter scale of cultural consequences—for anyone who noticed. The U.S. Supreme Court handed down its decision in the case of *Planned Parenthood of Southeastern Pennsylvania v. Casey, Governor of Pennsylvania*. In writing the majority opinion, Justices Sandra Day O'Connor, Souter, and Kennedy ruptured the bedrock of our culture when they proclaimed, "At the heart of liberty is the right to define one's own concept of existence, of meaning of the universe, and the mystery of human life."[127]

In saying so, the U.S. Supreme Court consecrated a contemptible worldview known as postmodernism. Postmodernism is the belief that truth and reality are not absolutes. Rather, they are "created" by each individual. This philosophy holds that two opposing truth claims can both be true—unless one of the claims is based on a morally absolute and "intolerant" worldview such as Christianity.

One person who noticed the desperate significance of this historic Supreme Court stance was Dr. James Dobson, president and founder of Focus on the Family. He warned:

> With those words, the Court discarded its historic reliance on "a law beyond the law," or a transcendent standard. The Founding Fathers based the Constitution on the understanding that human affairs are governed

by the moral law of the universe or what they termed "The Law of Nature and of Nature's God." That's why the Declaration of Independence reads, "All men are endowed by their Creator with certain unalienable Rights...."

Human dignity and freedom are precious gifts from God, rather than from government or its leaders. The Creator is also the ultimate definer of right and wrong. But after the *Casey* decision, this understanding of the moral absolutes was supplanted by "the right to define one's own concept of existence, of meaning of the universe and the mystery of human life."[128]

Columnist John Leo explained further the implications of the *Casey* ruling:

This "mystery passage'" [as it has become known] can be cited easily next time to justify suicide clinics, gay marriage, polygamy, inter-species marriage [such as marrying one's dog or cat] or whatever new individual right the court feels like inventing. We are moving firmly into the court's post-constitutional phase.[129]

Chuck Colson agrees, saying the mystery passage could mean absolutely anything to a future court, including the right to marry your toaster if you wish.[130]

James Dobson adds this summary analysis:

The bottom line of the *Casey* decision is how we define reality. The new definition flows from a "postmodern" philosophy that acknowledges nothing right nor wrong, nothing moral nor immoral. Truth does not exist and

there are no absolutes that transcend time. Everything is relative and subject to individual interpretation. For the U.S. Supreme Court to descend into this abyss of moral relativism is disastrous. The Constitution has been the shield, the defender, of basic liberties for 210 years based on "The Law of Nature and of Nature's God." Now, according to Justice Kennedy and five of his colleagues, its meaning has become nothing more predictable than the shifting sand of individual opinion.
131

There is nothing here based so much on a commitment to preserving political liberties as it is to anointing whatever demented lifestyles people may choose to pursue. Unlike the Supreme Court justices, our Founding Fathers knew what to call things that went against the Law of Nature and of Nature's God: sin. But if the postmodern worldview continues to gain acceptance by the courts, legislatures, and individual Americans, then it should be no surprise when politicians finally force us to accept partial-birth abortion, same-sex marriage, and sex with children as part of a person's right to live according to an individual definition of truth.

All of this brings to mind the words of King Solomon, who wrote in Proverbs 14:12, "There is a way that seems right to a man, but in the end it leads to death" (NIV).

NOTES

[1] Ken Ham, Jonathan Sarfati, Carl Weiland, *The Revised & Expanded Answers Book* (Green Forest, AR: Master Books, 1990), p. 17.

[2] Josh McDowell, *Christianity, Hoax or History* (Wheaton, IL: Pocket Guides, Tyndale House Publishers, Inc. , 1989), p. 83-84.

[3] *Time*, December 7, 1987

[4] Kevin Ryerson, *Spirit Communication: The Soul's Path* (New York: Bantam Books, 1989), p. 84.

[5] Dr. Dennis Cuddy, *Chronology of Education with Quotable Quotes* (Highland City, FL: Pro Family Forum Inc. 1993), p. 9.

[6] Governor Roy Romer while serving as Chairman of the National Governor's Association said this before an education meeting being covered by C-Span

[7] Brannon Howse, *No Retreats, No Reserves, No Regrets* (St. Paul, MN: Stewart House Press, 2000), p. 115.

[8] May 23, 1996, *The Cincinnati Post*

[9] March 16, 1992, *New York Times International.*

[10] This was from a conversation had with Mrs. Tucker when we testified before a Senate committee in Kansas on the dangers of School to Work.

[11] Aldous Huxley, *Brave New World.*

[12] In the February 4, 1998, issue of *Education Week*, Mark Tucker was quoted in an article written by Millicent Lawton.

[13] John J. Dunphy, "A Religion For A New Age," *Humanist magazine*, January/February 1983, p. 23-26.

[14] Charles Francis Potter, *Humanism: A New Religion* (New York: Simon & Schuster, 1930), p. 128.

[15] Paul C. Vitz, *Censorship: Evidence of Bias in Our Children's Textbooks* (Ann Arbor, MI: Servant Books, 1986), p. 2-3.

[16] Ibid.

[17] J.P. Moreland, editor, *The Creation Hypothesis*, "The Methodological Equivalence of Design and Descent: Can There Be a 'Scientific Theory of Creation?'" by S.C. Meyer (Downers Grove, IL: Intervarsity Press, 1994), p. 98.

[18] P.L. Tan, *Encyclopedia of 7700 illustrations : [a treasury of illustrations, anecdotes, facts and quotations for pastors, teachers and Christian workers]* (Garland, TX: Bible

Communications, 1996, c1979).

[19] Dr. Walter T. Brown, Jr., *In the Beginning* (Phoenix, AZ., 1989), p.2.

[20]P.L. Tan, *Encyclopedia of 7700 illustrations*.

[21] D.G. Lindsay, *Harmony of Science and Scripture* (Dallas: Christ for the Nations, 1998).

[22] Bill Gates, *The Road Ahead*, rev. ed. (New York: Penguin, 1996), p. 228.

[23] C.R. Darwin, *Origin of Species*, 6th edition, 1872 (London: John Murray, 1902), p. 413.

[24] Letter (written April 10, 1979) from Dr. Colin Patterson, then senior paleontologist at the British Museum of Natural History in London, to Luther D. Sunderland, as quoted in L.D. Sunderland, *Darwin's Enigma* (Green Forest, AR: Master Books, 1984), p. 89.

[25] Dr. Walter T. Brown Jr., *In the Beginning* (Phoenix, AZ: publisher, 1989), p.5-6.

[26] Oswald Spengler, *The Decline of the West*, Vol. 2 (New York: Alfred A. Knopf, 1966), p.32.

[27] *New York Sun*, February 12, 2008, Mayor Compares Threat of Global Warming to Terrorism.

[28] David Barton, Testimony before the U.S. Senate Hearing on Global Warming in the Environment and Public Works Committee, June 7, 2007.

[29] Ibid., p. 3

[30] Ibid.

[31] Ibid.

[32] Ibid.

[33] Tom DeWeese, *Fanatics, heretics and the truth about Global Warming*

[34] Ibid.

[35] Interview with Dr. S. Fred Singer, Nova, PBS, March 12, 2000.

[36] *News Week International*, Richard S. Lindzen, "Why So Gloomy", April 16, 2007.

[37] Tom DeWeese, *Fanatics, heretics and the truth about Global Warming*

[38] Ibid.

[39] Ibid.

[40] *February 13, 2008, Baliunas Says Global Warming Related to the Sun*, found at: http://www.tylerpaper.com/article/20080213/NEWS08/802130360

[41] David Barton, *Original Intent* (Aledo, TX: Wallbuilders Press, 1996), p. 17.

[42] William Blackstone, 1 Commentaries, *39, 41.

[43] James Wilson, *The Works of the Honourable James Wilson* Vol. I (Philadelphia:

Bronson and Chauncey, 1804), p. 106.

[44] Ibid.

[45] George Washington, Address of George Washington, President of the United States, and Late Commander in Chief of the American Army. To the People of the United States, Preparatory to His Declination (Baltimore: George and Henry S. Keating, 1796).

[46] John Jay, *The Correspondence and Public Papers of John Jay, 1794-1826*, Henry P. Johnson, Ed. (Reprint, NY: Burt Franklin, 1970), Vol. IV, p. 393, October 12, 1816.

[47] Tim LaHaye, David Noebel, *Mind Siege* (Nashville: Word Publishing, 2000), p. 187.

[48] George Grant, *The Family Under Siege*, p. 145.

[49] Ibid., p. 145, quoting Peggy Lamson, Roger Baldwin (Boston: Houghton Mifflin, 1976), p. 138-139.

[50] Ibid., p. 147.

[51] Ibid., p. 146.

[52] Letter by Thomas Jefferson to Danbury Baptist Association.

[53] David Barton, *The Foundations of American Government* (Aledo, TX: Wallbuilders Press, 1993), p. 5.

[54] Ibid., p. 41.

[55] Joseph Story, *Commentaries on the Constitution of the United States* (Boston: ___, 1833), II:593, quoted in Robert L. Cord, *Separation of Church and State: Historical Fact and Current Fiction* (New York: Lambeth Press, 1982), p. 731.

[56] Joseph Story, *Commentaries on the Constitution of the United States* (Boston: ___, 1833), II:593, quoted in Robert L. Cord, *Separation of Church and State: Historical Fact and Current Fiction* (New York: Lambeth Press, 1982), p. 13.

[57] Michael Drummond, *Participatory Democracy in the Making* (New York: Carnell, 1923), p. 19.

[58] Dr. John MacArthur, "Why Government Can't Save You," *An Alternative to Political Activism*, (Nashville, TN, Word Publishing, 2000), p. 6.

[59] David Barton "Was the American Revolution a Biblically Justified Act?" found at www.wallbuilders.com.

[60] Ibid.

[61] Barton, *Original Intent*, p. 337-8.

[62] Benjamin Rush, "A Defense of the Use of the Bible as a School Book, Addressed to the Rv. Jeremy Belknap, of Boston," *Essays, Literary, Moral and Philosophical* (Phila-

delphia: Thomas and Samuel F. Bradford, 1798), pp. 93-113.

[63] Noah Webster, *History of the United States* (New Haven: Durrie & Peck, 1832), p.6.

[64] Jedidiah Morse, "A Sermon, Exhibiting the Present Dangers and Consequent Duties of the Citizens of the United States of America," Delivered at Charlestown, April 25, 1799, *The Day of the National Fast* (Boston: Samuel Etheridge, 1799), p.11.

[65] *The Papers of James Madison*, Vol. III, Henry Gilpin, editor (Washington: Langtree and O'Sullivan, 1840), p. 1391, August 22, 1787.

[66] While the quote is attributed to Alexander Tyler, the Scottish history professor, this can not be proven even as researches have spent hours trying to confirm the source. While it may be a quote from Tyler, that can not be proven for certain.

[67] Ibid;

[68] Ibid.

[69] Ibid.

[70] Ibid.

[71] Charles Evans Hughes; quoted by Judge Brevard Hand, Wallace v. Jaffree, reversed, affirmed in part, 105 S. Ct. 2479 (1985).

[72] John Eidsmoe, *Christianity and the Constitution*, (Grand Rapids: Baker Book House, 1987), p.391.

[73] Ibid., p.394.

[74] Barton, *Original Intent*, p.228.

[75] Oliver Wendell Holmes, Jr., "The Law in Science-Science in Law," *Collected Legal Papers* (New York: Harcourt, Brace and Company, 1920), p. 225.

[76] Ibid., p. 220.

[77] Kerby Anderson, *Moral Dilemmas* (Nashville: Word Publishing, 1998), p. 221.

[78] Ibid., p. 220.

[79] Kerby Anderson, "A Biblical View of Economics," posted at probe.org.

[80] *What Does the Bible Say About—: The Ultimate A to Z Resource Fully Illustrated*, Nelson's A to Z Series (Nashville: Thomas Nelson, 2001), p. 272.

[81] From the website of Citizens Against Government Waste.

[82] Article by David Barton from his website wallbuilders.com.

[83] A government study cited online at rushlimbaugh.com.

[84] David Noebel, *The Battle For Truth* (Eugene, OR: Harvest House Publishers, 2001), p. 276.

[85] Rush Limbaugh, *See, I Told You So* (New York: Simon & Schuster, 1993), p.

78-80.

[86] Ibid.

[87] Kerby Anderson, *Moral Dilemmas* (Nashville: Word Publishing, 1998) p. 27-28.

[88] The Heartland Institute, 1993 report

[89] Southern Baptist Convention Kingdom Families International Literature.

[90] Ibid., p. ix.

[91] Ibid., p. x.

[92] Ibid., xi-xii.

[93] Charles Francis Potter, *Humanism,* p.128.

[94] Dunphy, "A Religion For A New Age"

[95] Brooks Alexander, "The Rise of Cosmic Humanism: What is Religion?" SCP Journal (Vol. 5, Winter 1981-82) p. 1992.

[96] Television news interview program in which Senator Peter Hoagland was interviewed. Brannon Howse has a recording of this interview.

[97] Vitz, *Censorship,* p. 2-3.

[98] Ibid.

[99] Ibid.

[100] "Religion," *Webster's New World Dictionary of the English Language—The Unabridged Edition* (New York: Random House, Inc., 1966, 1973), 135.

[101] "Belief," *The Random House Dictionary of the English Language—The Unabridged Editions* (New York: Random House, Inc., 1966, 1973), 135.

[102] Tim LaHaye and David Noebel, *Mind Siege: The Battle for Truth in the New Millennium* (Nashville, TN: Word Publishing, 2000), quoting Ian S. Markham, ed., *A World Religions Reader,* 2nd ed. (Malden, MA: Blackwell Publishers, 2000).

[103] David Noebel, *Clergy in the Classroom* (Manitou Springs, CO: Summit Press, 1995), 9.

[104] *Torcaso vs. Watkins,* 367 U.S. 488, 495, fn. 11 (1961)

[105] Ibid.

[106] David Noebel, *The Battle for Truth* (Eugene, OR: Harvest House Publishers, 2001), 37.

[107] Brannon Howse, *Reclaiming a Nation at Risk* (Chandler, AZ, Bridgestone Multimedia, 1995), p. 112.

[108] Laura Rogers, "In Loco Parentis: The Brave New Family in Missouri," *Freedom Report*, February 1993, p. 15.

[109] *Education Week*, March 11, 1992.

[110] Thomas Sowell, *Inside American Education* (New York: Free Press, 1993), p. 51.

[111] Ibid.

[112] George Grant, *Grand Illusions: The Legacy of Planned Parenthood* (Franklin, TN: Adroit Press, 1993), p. 53.

[113] Ibid.

[114] George Grant, *The Family Under Siege: What the New Social Engineers Have in Mind for You and Your Children* (Minneapolis, MN: Bethany House Publishers, 1994), p. 59.

[115] Ibid., p. 61.

[116] Ibid., p. 62.

[117] Ibid.

[118] Margaret Sanger, "The Case for Birth Control: A Supplementary Brief and Statement of Facts" (New York: Eugenic Publishing Company, 1917), p. 3.

[119] Ibid., p. 105.

[120] Ibid., p. 88.

[121] Ibid., p. 165.

[122] Grant, *The Family Under Siege*, p. 62.

[123] *Planned Parenthood Federation of America Service Report 1992*, p. 3.

[124] Paul Copan, *True for You, But not for Me* (Minneapolis, MN: Bethany House Publishers, 1998), p.32-33. Cites D.A. Carson, *The Sermon on the Mount* (Grand Rapids, MI: Baker, 1978), 97.

[125] Roger Rosenblat, "God Is Not on My Side. Or Yours," *Time*, Dec. 17, 2001, p. 92.

[126] Stanley J. Grenz, *A Primer on Postmodernism* (Grand Rapids, MI: William B. Eerdmans Publishing Company), p. 14.

[127] *Family News from Dr. James Dobson* (Colorado Springs: Focus on the Family, October 1997).

[128] Ibid.

[129] John Leo, "In the Matter of the Court vs. Us," *U.S. News and World Report*, October 7, 1996, p. 28.

[130] Chuck Colson, "Pandora's Box," *BreakPoint*, March 11, 1996.

[131] *Family News from Dr. James Dobson*

About the Author

Brannon Howse is president and founder of American Family Policy Institute and Worldview Weekend, America's largest Christian worldview conference series. Founded in 1993, Worldview Weekend is now held in more than twenty states each year with an annual attendance of approximately 20,000 to 25,000. Brannon is also:

- Founder of www.christianworldviewnetwork.com, which features columns and articles by some of America's best Christian worldview authors and speakers.

- Founder of *Worldview Weekend* Online Institute (www.worldviewtraining.com), a 12-week online course exploring the Biblical worldview. The course is also available as in-class curriculum featuring leader and student manuals, DVDs, CDs, and tests.

- A trained tenor soloist who has performed in hundreds of American churches as well as at the Anaheim Convention Center for 10,000 delegates of the Association of Christian Schools International.

- Host of the Worldview Weekend Family Reunion held in Branson, Missouri, each spring and attended by more than 2,000 people. The three-day event features nationally known speakers, comedians, and musicians.

- A researcher for the White House Office of Faith-Based Ministries as well as best-selling authors Michael Reagan, Josh McDowell, and David Limbaugh.

• The education reporter and frequent guest host for *The Michael Reagan Show*.

• Author of eight books on education, family issues, and Christian, including *An Educational Abduction, Reclaiming a Nation at Risk, One Nation Under Man?: The Worldview War Between Christians and the Secular Left, Christian Worldview for Students, Christian Worldview for Children, Building a Biblical Worldview Verse by Verse, Put Your Beliefs to the Test,* and *Christian Worldview for Students Volume II.*

• President of Worldview Weekend Publishing.

• Host of the daily radio program, *Worldview Matters,* and host of *Christian Worldview This Week,* a weekly radio broadcast heard on more than 225 stations each week.

• A periodic guest on over 800 radio and television programs, including *The O'Reilly Factor* (Fox News), *The News on MSNBC, Truths That Transform with Dr. D. James Kennedy, The G. Gordon Liddy Show, The Michael Reagan Show, The Ken Hamblin Show, The Oliver North Show, Action Sixties, Point of View, Family News and Focus, U.S.A. Radio News,* and *Standard News.*

ABOUT WORLDVIEW
WEEKEND CONFERENCES

Christians today are bombarded with information and opinions by the media, schools, and government. No one can hope to assimilate the avalanche of data. So who could possibly understand the times in which we live? Not many! But those men and women who do become the next generation of leaders.

The Bible speaks of a small tribe in Israel that "understood the times" and knew "what Israel ought to do," and as a result, they became leaders (1 Chronicles 12:32). God expects His people to seek earnestly for the truth, rewarding with greater responsibility those who comprehend. Worldview Weekend Conferences are dedicated to teaching you how to understand our times and grasp the opportunity that will give you for leadership.

Worldview Weekend features nationally known speakers such as David Limbaugh, David Barton, Kirk Cameron, David Jeremiah, Kerby Anderson, Star Parker, Ken Ham, Erwin Lutzer and others.

The recommended age of attendance is age 11 to adult. Worldview Weekend sponsors a one-night event know as a Code Blue Rally. These free, one-night events are held in numerous states each year.

To find out more about how to attend the Worldview Weekend of your choice, go to www.worldviewweekend.com

WORLDVIEW
WEEKEND RESOURCES

We invite you to take advantage of these helpful
Worldview Weekend Resources:

- Visit worldviewweekend.com and check out the **Berean Club.**
  You can load more than 125 Worldview Weekend keynote
  presentations onto your ipod, listen online or burn a cd.

- Further your worldview knowledge by taking our online course,
  Developing a Christian Worldview. Try our free demo at
  worldviewtraining.com

- We have DVDs featuring *Kirk Cameron, Ray Comfort, David Barton,
  Josh McDowell, Sean McDowell* and others. Check out our books
  and DVDs in our bookstore at worldviewweekend.com

- Visit christianworldviewnetwork.com for daily news and
  columns from a Biblical worldview perspective.

- Brannon's book, ***One Nation Under Man? The Worldview War
  Between Christians and the Secular Left***, can be purchased from
  our online bookstore at worldviewweekend.com.